Corporate Accountability and Trust
Thoughts from 12 Top Managers

Mazars is an international organisation specialised in auditing and consulting services to companies. Mazars federates 13,000 people around the world, operating in 58 countries.

Because individual and collective responsibility is at the heart of its profession, Mazars has assembled this book in order to promote and enrich the corporate responsibility debate.

Mazars wishes to express its thanks to Jean-Philippe Daniel and Nicolas Daniels for their collaboration in carrying out the interviews.

www.mazars.com

Corporate Accountability and Trust
Thoughts from 12 Top Managers

Under the direction of Patrick de Cambourg

MAZARS

ECONOMICA

49, rue Héricart, 75015 Paris

Interviews prepared and carried out by Jean-Philippe Daniel and Nicolas Daniels.

Project coordinated by the Corporate Communications Department of Mazars: Muriel Bachelier, Head of Corporate Communications, Valérie Lonchampt (art direction), Catherine Zang, Delphine Bieth, Dany Sok

Translated from the French by JAM Translations.

Photo credits: Getty Images

Printing: November 2006

For their active participation, we express our thanks to:

César Alierta,
Chairman and CEO of Telefónica

Alessandro Benetton,
Vice President of the Board of Directors of Benetton Group S.p.A

Martin Bouygues,
Chairman and CEO of Bouygues Group

Patrick de Cambourg,
Chairman of the Group Executive Board of Mazars

Henri de Castries,
Chairman of the Management Board of AXA

Alain Etchegoyen,
Philosopher

Adi Godrej,
Chairman and CEO of the Godrej Group

Stephen Green,
Chairman and Executive Director of the HSBC Group

Daniel Janssen,
Chairman of the Board of Directors of Solvay

Professor Gilbert Lenssen,
President of EABIS

Nicole Notat,
President of Vigeo

Martin Roman,
Chairman and CEO of ČEZ

Arun Sarin,
CEO of Vodafone

Ernest-Antoine Seillière,
President of the Supervisory Board of Wendel Investissement

Pierre Tapie,
President of the ESSEC Business School

Werner Wenning,
Chairman of the Board of Management of Bayer AG

Yang Yuanqing,
Chairman of the Board of Lenovo

FOREWORD

On Responsibility

Responsibility is today a catchword, of which French 20th-century poet and critic Paul Valéry stated they have *more value than meaning*. This particular fate produces multiple misuses and arbitrary contractions. For example, we hear that the tsunami is "responsible" for thousands of deaths. Given the tsunami's lack of self-awareness, we may speak of a "cause," but never responsibility – although causality is one aspect of responsibility. Similarly, since the denunciation in France of the *"petits chefs"* ("little bosses," or office tyrants) in 1968, we speak of the *"responsable"* of a workshop or a factory. This term encompasses the idea of power over a territory, but responsibility is not limited to this as there is a difference between being *"un responsable"* and being responsible – although power is one element in the concept of responsibility.

We are not condemning the use of a catchword. But understanding of the word is often marred by confusion of its various meanings. Responsibility is an emerging principle, without a doubt the moral principle of our era. Nonetheless, representations of responsibility are ambiguous, paradoxical and even contradictory. Two particular considerations support this statement.

Professional and private uses

First, the word is not limited to business use; it is not an obvious term in the managerial lexicon. The responsibility principle involves numerous spheres of our existence: private, professional, political. As the head of a household, as a manager or decision maker, as a citizen or elected official, I can be described as *responsible*. One of the major difficulties in our developed societies lies in the discontinuity between very different roles: often fully accountable at home, the same individual may not be considered so in his or her professional life.

Contradictory or paradoxical definitions?

Second, the word issues from a dual evolution which affects its meanings and connotations. Before examining this in detail, we can illustrate this divergence by comparing two brief, common expressions: on the one hand, the question *Who is responsible?*; on the other, the command to *Be responsible*. The first is legal; the second, moral, in nature.

The question *Who is responsible?* is posed after a disaster, a catastrophe or a defeat. Pell-mell: the Union Carbide catastrophe in India, the "mad cow" affair in Europe, or the defeat of a national sporting team. Something bad happens, an accident, and newspaper headlines are accusing: Who caused this damage? We look for those responsible. When the national team wins, the question is no longer posed. Useless to seek them out, so numerous are those who claim the honour of victory. In the French language, the causal relationship can be expressed in two ways: *à cause de (because of)* or *grâce à (thanks to)*. The question *Who is responsible?* is asked only in the first instance.

On the other hand, the command *Be responsible* represents a moral exhortation. We address it to our children, our students, to all those in whom we wish to instil moral behaviour.

In each case, the notion of responsibility evokes a very different image: bad on the one hand, good on the other. And yet it is the same word. These different usages should be kept in mind, as they allow us to understand why some seek out responsibility while others flee it: perhaps they do not have the same perception of the word.

We see this every day in the delegation of responsibility in companies. Either it represents an empowering process (positive), or the desire to find a scapegoat in case of problems (negative). All parents of school-age children are familiar with this little phrase which appears in paperwork distributed at the start of the school year and which fully encompasses the ambiguous meaning of responsibility: *if you are responsible parents, please ensure the responsibility...*

Powerful legal roots

The question *Who is responsible?* is not random. The notion of responsibility first developed in the legal tradition. And whatever the texts – the Civil Code, Penal Code, Urban Code etc. – responsibility refers only to condemnable actions. The person *responsible* has always harmed someone, caused an accident or damage: the law of responsibility is one of reparation.

We would be wrong to condemn this negative vision of responsibility. In fact, the law of responsibility represents considerable progress in our civilization, as it replaces vengeance. This latter contains elements of passion and affect whose roots reach down to the depths of human nature: we have only to evoke the numerous novels or films whose plots rely on this theme to convince ourselves – from *The Count of Monte-Cristo* to *Once Upon a Time in the West*, and including *The Godfather* and *Superman II*, vengeance provides a feeling of satisfaction to which no one is immune.

With the law of responsibility, I no longer evaluate the damage and resulting punishment myself; I leave this role to an external, neutral and objective judge. However, this progress still weighs on the notion of responsibility. In the name of better principles, we constantly seek out those who are responsible, to keep people from being alone in their suffering and to ensure that they receive compensation from the *responsible* party. We are progressively rejecting the very idea of an accident – *accidit* meaning "it happens", with a neutral subject; that is, no subject – preferring always to make someone responsible, especially in the context of the rapid growth of the judiciary which characterizes our developed societies.

The historical weight of these legal roots often muddies our view of responsibility. It can lead to inaction through fear of being designated responsible, especially when the basis for responsibility shifts from fault to risk in order to increase solidarity with the victims. This idea of responsibility without fault, anchored in jurisprudence, profoundly affects numerous professions, primarily medicine, politics and administration, and the upper echelons of business.

More recent moral roots

The moral tradition is far more recent. Hans Jonas's book *The Imperative of Responsibility*, published some thirty years ago in Germany, examined the moral dimension.

Curiously, while the word is the same, its meaning is almost flipped around to become its own opposite. Literally, the etymology – *respondeo*, in Latin, means to respond – gives its meaning to the concept: to be responsible is to "respond," or in English *to answer for* one's actions or decisions and their consequences. In the legal framework, I am required to respond, as in the witness stand. In the moral version, I want to respond; I make a commitment. To take responsibility is to want to respond; in other words, my duty is defined by this very desire. I know I must act, when I take responsibility or am offered it. I am thus incited to action, whereas the legal dimension most often incites me not to act.

After the *autonomy* movement – etymologically, *auto-nomos, to follow one's own law* – responsibility introduces the presence of the other as a decisive element. Indeed, if I respond, it is because someone, this other, implicitly or explicitly asks me a question. In the legal perspective, responsibilities must always be measured a priori; hence the multiplication of signs posted in parking lots, coat rooms or hotels: *management declines all responsibility*…In contrast, moral responsibility cannot be boxed up in this way. It is undefined without the presence of the other. Only the other gives it meaning. There may of course often be multiple others. For a company's board of directors, or its chief executive, five agents are present: suppliers, clients, employees, shareholders and society ("society" taking into account factors such as employment, the environment and security). This otherness creates distinct duties which may sometimes not converge. It is the role of the responsible party to arbitrate when taking decisions.

The ingredients of moral responsibility

We have already glimpsed two ingredients which have been mistreated: causality and power. I am responsible for an act or decision only if I carry it out or cause it. In this case, I must have certain power over a territory. If the territory is an empty shell, I am not responsible for anything. Company management was faced with this question with the advent of Taylorism, when attempting to give each worker power over a specific area: we observed this, for example, in the total-quality policies which marked the transition from management control to self-control. But the territory also cannot be infinite or undefined. I cannot be responsible for everything. This is why the boundaries of the territory are important. They are directly related to the others who impose themselves on those responsible.

Furthermore, the force of the moral imperative of responsibility resides in its *formal* and *universal* character. The responsibility principle is defined by a test which is applicable in every case. This formal test is not abstract. On the contrary. We live in an era in which new situations arise. We must improvise responses which are not transmitted to us by tradition or education – this is as true of globalization for companies as of the decomposing/recomposing of families. The principle of responsibility constitutes a new *North Star* in turbulent times.

The company, a forum for exemplary practice

The test Hans Jonas proposes is simple and clear. When faced with a decision or an action, I can always ask myself the following question: for this decision, this action and their consequences, do I want to give an accounting to others who are affected?

Let us take two examples, the actions of Francis Mer and Pierre Guillaumat. The former, when president of Pont-à-Mousson, decides to close a modern factory at Saint-Priest. All of his advisors recommend against his visiting there: he would be sequestered by the union (the *CGT*), the Human Resources Director or the factory manager could take care of the matter. Francis Mer retorts: I made the decision, it is up to me to answer for it to those concerned. He goes to the factory. He enters, surrounded by the union's pickets, suffers through a few unpleasant remarks as expected, but exits freely, because the demonstrators are so impressed by his courage and personal commitment.

In the early 1980s, Pierre Péan reveals the sniffer plane affair in *Le Monde*. Pierre Guillaumat, former Armed Forces Minister under General Charles de Gaulle, founder of Elf-Aquitaine, publishes a communiqué in every newspaper a few days later: "I was the boss, and therefore responsible, I will not tolerate that a single one of my subordinates be worried!" The dignity and elegance of these gestures subsumes them under the responsibility principle. They highlight a fundamental ingredient of responsibility: courage. We see this in two essential questions which follow.

Does responsibility imply disobedience?

A tendency exists among many who study the concept of responsibility to reply to the question *Who is the other?* with "It is the Boss." Each person would be considered to be responsible first to the hierarchical superior. Reducing the other to this individual, however important, leads to a questionable limitation of the concept of responsibility. In fact, responsibility is thus eroded, slowly but surely, into a degraded concept which is merely a new version of obedience.

However, responsibility, along with the courage which accompanies it, can invite or even incite to disobedience. Even the regulations of the Armed Forces contain this duty of disobedience in the name of responsibility. The most flagrant historic example is that of General de Gaulle: the call of June 18 is a manifesto of the responsibility which is expressed in disobedience. This situation is not rare within companies.

We must acknowledge that, in contrast to a conformist morality – we speak often of the *moral order* – responsibility is a subversive principle. It leads to improvisation, inventiveness and innovation in approaching the many moral questions which arise in the economic sphere.

Can we say that we have no choice?

The second question concerns rhetoric which is flourishing in the discourse of our leaders. The argument developed during a difficult decision is summarized as follows: we don't have the choice, it's globalization, only one decision was possible. This rhetoric is contrary to the principle of responsibility. In this context, the principle is a modern avatar of the great debate presented by the Stoics. For them, the major questions were: *what is under our control?* and *what is not under our control?* Thus, nominating the management of my company is under my control. Globalization is not under my control. But the Stoics added a fundamental detail: my attitude to that which is not under my control is entirely under my control. We will all die – death is not under our control – but we can control our attitude towards death; the same is true of major decisions which commit the responsibility of our leaders. To deny the existence of a choice is to refuse to take responsibility for our decisions. Indeed, a manager who claims that no other decision is possible should be immediately replaced: what use is he, if he makes no choice? This rhetoric evades the test of the responsibility principle.

Diffusing the principle of responsibility

We do not need a university degree in philosophy to intuitively understand responsibility. Any parents who have held their newborn in their arms has perceived its meaning. Whether the birth resulted from a desire for children or a mistake in timing, the responsibility remains the same. Hans Jonas calls this *natural responsibility*. He distinguishes it from *contractual responsibility*, which results from a decision: I accept, I take responsibility for a company, a service, a community, etc. The decision, if it does not arise merely from an appetite for power, if it is based on the content of the responsibility principle itself, will serve to disseminate this principle.

A modern form of autocracy consists of concentrating power and responsibility in a single hand. But responsibility is a double risk which I take: to be responsible, but also to ensure the accountability of those people whose errors or faults would be attributed to me. Responsibility is not taught didactically, but must be transmitted through its exercise.

Let us consider an analogy with which all parents are familiar. One day, we let our child run an errand alone. We are anxious, we give careful directions, we watch from the window, we see her cross the street, we are uneasy... but we know we must do it; she will never grow up if we are always there to hold her hand. Responsibility is a risk. But to give responsibility is also a risk. It is the humanist risk which we must take, if we truly believe that humankind has innate value.

Alain Etchegoyen,
philosopher

INTRODUCTION

Any consideration of corporate responsibility leads to an examination of the role which the company must play in today's society. It is precisely the desire to make our contribution to this debate which led to Mazars's decision to launch this book. The approach was self-evident: invite top managers in Europe and Asia to directly express how they perceive their organisation's responsibility and their own responsibility as top executives. Why choose European and Asian companies? Because we thought it would be enlightening to address the issue of responsibility with a view that is not directly affected by American standards, as they appear to be implemented, notably through the Sarbanes-Oxley Act[1]. Are there other possible approaches, other cultures of responsibility? This is the question. The collected testimonials, to which we have added contributions from qualified personalities – French philosopher Alain Etchegoyen, president of the Vigeo social rating agency Nicole Notat, president of Essec Pierre Tapie, and European Academy for Business in Society president Gilbert Lenssen – make up a publication which is both rich in ideas and thought-provoking. A publication true to Mazars's citizen spirit.

Corporate social responsibility is certainly not a new phenomenon. Among the large corporate CEOs who have done us the honour of contributing to this book, several are heirs to longstanding industrial dynasties and refer to the "paternalistic capitalism" which reigned within a given city or region beginning in the late 19th century, in

---

1. The Sarbanes-Oxley Act was signed into law on 30th July 2002 by the President of the United States of America, and entails highly significant legislative changes to financial practice and corporate governance regulation for all companies listed on the US Stock Exchange. It introduces stringent new rules with the stated objective: "to protect investors by improving the accuracy and reliability of corporate disclosures made pursuant to the securities laws."

which the lives of workers and their families were almost completely taken charge of by their employer. In the euphoria of the Industrial Revolution, whose limits were not yet apparent, certain capitalists considered this social commitment to be both a moral obligation, often with a strong religious foundation, and the best way to ensure the permanence of their workforce over several generations. At Michelin, for example, sons followed in their fathers' footsteps as workers, then foremen and sometimes engineers.

A hundred years down the road, the rules of the game have changed. Large corporations are international. Their managers and employees come from different countries and often different continents; their clients and customers as well. In addition, as Martin Bouygues points out in his essay, the accountability of managers and of companies has been affected by three major catalysts over the past fifty years: the emergence and growth at the international level of the consumer movement which emerged in the United States, the development of legislation to regulate relations between companies and their employees, and the increasing weight of shareholders, which modifies the relationship between a group's management and its owners.

A global market, better-informed and more demanding consumers, better-protected employees, more influential shareholders: all of these contribute to greater corporate accountability. This "new deal" is further affected, owing to the multiplication of information sources, stronger pressure from public opinion and, in the wake of certain scandals, more vigilance on the part of regulators, whose demands in terms of reliability of financial and extra-financial information have required companies to implement significant efforts.

Are these evolutions positive, or do they represent a set of constraints which are too heavy? As always, it is best to remain balanced.

As a number of executives express in no uncertain terms in their contributions, companies are a powerful motor for the creation of wealth and the mobilization of resources, and should therefore pre-serve their freedom and autonomy. Nonetheless, they are also legal entities which, in exchange for this autonomy, must respect their commitments, to their "owners" first of all, whether these are a family, a group of individuals or a large number of shareholders. In this context, it seems natural that those holding capital be able to sanction, if necessary, managers who they consider in one way or another to have failed at their task and endangered the company's long-term existence. As many of the CEOs interviewed in this book also highlight, the responsibility of the groups they manage must also be towards all those with whom they have developed relations, whether contractual or not. There is, to my mind, nothing shocking about this.

I consider first the employees. Beyond the legal protections which apply to them, it seems to me that companies have a duty to provide employees with the best conditions for accomplishing their tasks, and, indeed, for their own personal development. Alessandro Benetton and Adi Godrej in particular stress this fundamental aspect of the company's role and the implied necessary investments, which are sometimes in opposition to purely financial considerations. This is also what we aim to implement at Mazars: to give all our associates the possibility of progressing and of participating, when the time comes, in ownership of the company.

Next, I think of clients. A company has no meaning without its clients – or rather, its clientele; that is, its current and potential clients. They have legitimate and growing demands for quality and, in the case of consumers, for information about the origin and manufacturers of products which are offered to them. This irreversible evolution, born of the consumer movements mentioned above and amplified by generalized access to information, must be seen as a major factor for progress for all parties concerned.

I consider, finally, the company's environment, in the broad sense: its suppliers, government authorities, regulators and, more generally, the whole of civil society. I believe that in this area, it would be excessive to lay responsibility on companies which would create focal points too separate from the overall organisation of socio-political life. We must remember that the company's primary mission is to create products and services (and thus wealth) through economic and financial mechanisms.

Entrepreneurship contributes, in my opinion, to the positive evolution of society. I am convinced that in this matter, the opposition between liberalism, in which the entrepreneur has full power, and a vision in which, in contrast, the well-being of man and society takes priority, is largely theoretical, as surely the most uncontrolled liberalism could not succeed without the support of society and thus of citizens. This is why I believe companies are always, to some degree, indebted to their social and societal environment and that they must, from this perspective, contribute to its improvement. Many concrete examples are cited in this book: education for Wendel Investissement, Telefónica and Solvay, cultural philanthropy for AXA, and environmental initiatives for Vodafone, among others.

These expectations of companies in the social, environmental and societal spheres are, once again, justified.

Nonetheless, in terms of governance and relations with regulators, we must take care that they do not mutate into too difficult a weight to carry. It is normal that companies communicate and give an account to stakeholders; it is excessive to ask that they submit to regulations which could, at times, endanger the very possibility of enterprise and development. To support each and every person's sense of responsibility, as well as transparency: this is the challenge.

An example, mentioned in the interviews and of which my profession makes me particularly aware, is that of transparency of financial information. I would like to mention two main points, one concerning Mazars, the other more general.

Professional firms such as Mazars have long maintained a tradition of confidentiality. Their ownership and rules of operation were often considered to belong to the private sphere. We believe this is an outmoded tradition. This is why we have communicated about ourselves, so that those we serve know with whom they are working. It is a serious exercise based on the idea that a service's value is defined by its content, but also, in the area of intangible services, by who delivers it. Recently, we decided to continue this philosophy to its logical end by voluntarily submitting to the discipline of an Annual Report and by producing, at the group level, financial information audited according to the strictest standards (IFRS). We were in no way obliged to publish this document, but it seemed indispensable to us to apply to ourselves the discipline which, as auditors, we help apply to our clients.

That a company reliably communicate its results, its financial situation, its management and governance structure is therefore indispensable. It is necessary for all stakeholders. It seems perfectly logical that the modalities for this be set out in a legal framework. However, we must ensure that legal provisions do not extend their requirements too far: on the one hand, because this would remove accountability from the actors, who would merely be performing a "box ticking" exercise, and on the other hand because, as Alessandro Benetton points out, we would end up stacking unwieldy and costly demands on companies which, for the most part, have a primary responsibility to create enough profit to pay their employees and maintain the jobs which they have created. In this context, the current debate in the United States about the application of the Sarbanes-Oxley Act to the smallest listed companies is revealing.

A word, before concluding, on executives' personal responsibility. All CEOs interviewed for this book have an elevated conception of their role, which they take on with pride, humility and full consciousness of the implications of their decisions. All testify to a strong personal commitment to respecting the rules of governance, to the professional development of the men and women whom they manage and to the necessary acceptance by all of common values and rules of conduct, in initiatives taken by their company in social, educational, cultural or environmental matters.

While this commitment is also my own, I also firmly believe in the need to teach. By teaching, I understand, the ability to explain, but also to listen, to ensure that there is sufficient consensus within the company, between the company and its markets and between the company and society, to justify the pursuit of its development.

We must, to my mind, avoid sanctifying managers, not give in to the temptation of celebrity. When a company and its managers respect their workers, their clients and their environment, circles of trust are created. The multiplication of these circles of trust is one of the conditions for the survival and development of what remains an entrepreneurial adventure, or quite simply a human adventure, whatever the rules applied.

Patrick de Cambourg,
Chairman of the Group Executive Board of Mazars

César Alierta
Chairman and CEO of Telefónica

"Corporate responsibility is above all a matter of free will."

To whom and how are today's companies accountable?

The current debate about corporate social responsibility centres on this question exactly: who is responsible for what, and to whom? This is a trend which has been emerging in recent years owing to a number of factors: globalization, corporate governance scandals, increasing interest on the part of citizens and a desire to be better informed... One of the most important elements has doubtless been the privatization of numerous companies, which has led to a radical change in the economic and social landscape.

To answer the question, I believe that a company's primary responsibility is to do what it does *well*, and in compliance with existing laws. Beyond this necessary respect for regulations, the only thing a company has to offer its stakeholders is a promise to strive for excellence. This is how Telefónica approaches corporate responsibility. It is a deliberate choice made by the company to improve relations with its stakeholders through a better understanding of their expectations and by taking these into account in daily management decisions.

Thus, when we speak of responsibility, we should not frame the concept in terms of accusations or assignment of guilt, but rather as an indication of the attention we pay to our decisions and undertakings.

To whom are we responsible? I believe that companies have learned a crucial lesson: our survival depends on the relations we are able to maintain with our stakeholders. It is inconceivable for a company to succeed today if it does not earn the confidence of its clients, employees, suppliers and shareholders.

**As the top manager of a major corporation,
how do you personally experience this responsibility?**

I am proud of this role and work to share it with the entire management team. Responsibility must be transmitted through every organizational level so that each person does his or her part. In the end, corporate responsibility at Telefónica is a process, which must be present in each and every decision made by and for the company.

In a company of 200,000 employees, one of the most important challenges we must meet is that of creating and transmitting a common culture. We must ensure that all of our employees, individually and together, feel proud to work for Telefónica. This is a first example which nicely illustrates how we live out corporate responsibility.

The second example which I would like to mention relates to our approach to diversity. Telefónica is present in numerous countries with different cultures, and aims everywhere to be locally anchored. We strive to be Brazilian in Brazil, Peruvian in Peru and Spanish in Spain. We always keep in mind that our corporate culture must respect the social and societal cultures and traditions of the countries in which we operate. This is how we ensure our enduring welcome.

In addition, I believe that managers of large companies must exercise social responsibility in their role as employers, not only towards their own employees but also – because they are an example for future generations – towards those who are students today. This is without doubt an important responsibility.

Finally, we are at the helm of companies which are motors for innovation, equal opportunity and the economic development of certain countries. As such, it behoves us to manage them in such a way that they produce benefits for society as a whole. This, too, is a heavy responsibility.

**What concrete changes has the emergence of Corporate
Responsibility brought about in your company?
And what further changes are to come?**

Obligations arising from corporate responsibility may vary from one country to another. These national differences are mainly attributable to the degree of legislative involvement, not only in relations between the company and its stakeholders, but also in terms of broader social responsibility. Countries such as the United Kingdom or Denmark, for example, have laws and government policies which promote and provide a framework for corporate responsibility.

From a more general point of view, the current situation leads us to ask a fundamental question, and also raises a paradox: if we are talking about controls and regulations, at what level should they be set? Is it possible to put into place a single global model which would keep national initiatives from diverging too widely and definitions from becoming confused? Many countries are examining their regulations individually. To arrive at an overall agreement will necessitate the definition of minimal standards. But we must not forget that corporate responsibility is above all a matter of free will, which means that excessive regulation would work against the ultimate goal.

From the company's point of view, we should remember that corporate responsibility is also a catalyst for internal change and transformation. We conceive of corporate responsibility as described above; that is, as a path to excellence. Specific changes will thus be those which each company makes of its own volition.

How are these changes beneficial to today's companies?

A number of factors today have a strong impact on corporate action, and this is a fundamental change. Opinions expressed by "interest groups", their requests for information, the ways in which the media now cover topics related to companies' behaviour... All of these elements are contributing to a radical change in management models and concepts of leadership.

But the most important change is that we live today in an era of transparency. Consumers, shareholders, employees and society as a whole want to know not only how much money a company is earning, but also how it is earned. This is a small revolution, and at Telefónica we are ready to welcome it and accept the consequences.

How would you rate the public image of companies and CEOs in today's society?

In the wake of the recent scandals in corporate governance, companies certainly do not enjoy a high level of confidence from society as a whole... but I believe this situation is beginning to change.

One of the most significant indicators of this turnaround is the fact that companies are learning, little by little, to work with their interest groups. Today, companies consult with stakeholders or their representatives and consider this input when making important decisions. Complex partnership projects are even created between companies and their stakeholders.

It is in companies' interest to continue along this path. A firm's relations with its stakeholders is an important element in its evaluation by socially responsible investors, who are key actors today. And if this also allows us to improve management, why not?

It is my belief that we are on the right path, one which will allow us to earn trust once again. But there is much left to do.

Alessandro Benetton
Vice-President of the Board of Directors of Benetton
Group S.p.A

"A question of principles and personal responsibility."

To whom and how are today's companies accountable?

The list of people and organizations for which a company carries responsibility is a long one. It includes above all employees, clients, shareholders, suppliers and other business relations, but also its immediate environment, the city in which it is located and, in the case of large companies, society as a whole. Such responsibility creates a paradox, as the interests of these different parties could be in conflict. A company's efforts in favour of one group may be detrimental to others, and vice versa. The necessity of constantly balancing these various interests requires an active will on all sides, not just that of the company, to reach compromises.

In formal terms, responsibility is expressed in its broadest sense by the respect for a set of rules – a relatively large set in Benetton's case, as we are listed on the New York Stock Exchange. We are thus subject to the terms of the Sarbanes-Oxley law which regulate accounting transparency and the transmission of financial information. We take great care in fulfilling these obligations, as we always have. Benetton has long been a company with irreproachable management, and has repeatedly earned recognition for its performance in this area.

However, I would like to start off by pointing out a paradox. Of course these rules are useful and fully justified, particularly to avoid repeating scandals such as the Enron affair, and we respect regulations with this in mind. I would even venture that Benetton is fairly advanced and has adopted the most rigorous standards. That being said, I believe we must examine with care the weight of the regulatory yoke being created. It should not limit entrepreneurial freedom or the growth of companies, and thus of the economy as a whole. It should also not be detrimental to the individual responsibility and creative spirit which are vital to the success of a company.

While the accumulation of regulations can create problems, it is not a very significant issue for a company the size of Benetton. We have the resources to meet these requirements. But we must keep in mind that 95% of companies are small or medium-sized. They have very concrete concerns: being paid by their clients and paying their employees at the end of each month. If they are overloaded with regulatory obligations, these are met at the expense of their business. This is particularly damaging in that these companies' primary responsibility, from a social perspective, is to create and preserve jobs.

Once again, I am not rejecting the rules, especially for large companies. I simply think it is an error to believe they will suffice. Recent history shows that we can always find ways to get around rules. Responsibility is above all a personal issue. It is best to define a framework and principles, because principles do not leave loopholes.

As the top manager of a major corporation, how do you personally experience this responsibility?

I belong to a generation for which managers' responsibility has become self-evident. I remember when I was in the Harvard MBA program in 1989, an optional class on the ethics of management and business was offered to students for the first time. At the time, this was a quasi-revolutionary step. Today, it has become a required class in every student's curriculum. What was previously not a major concern, for managers or for society in general, appears to have become one today.

Of course this doesn't mean that unethical behaviour was tolerated, but simply that a sense of responsibility was perceived as belonging to the personal sphere. What has changed in recent years is that, owing to a greater social and environmental consciousness, and also because of the scandals mentioned earlier, ethical requirements for management practices are today at the centre of public debate.

In the case of Benetton, however, the "citizenship" role of the company and its managers has been evident for a number of years. In 1987, in our immediate environment in Treviso, we created the Benetton Foundation, which sponsors projects related to landscape management, the history of the Veneto region and the history of games.

Locally, Benetton is also a sponsor for rugby, basketball and volleyball teams which regularly win Italian championships.

Internationally, Benetton and its leaders are often active in campaigns carried out by the UN and its various agencies, and also work with associations such as Amnesty International or SOS Racisme. More than a simple slogan, the United Colors of Benetton expresses a very real attitude and a commitment to concrete action on the part of the group's management.

Do you believe today's top executives have to lead by example, vis-à-vis their employees and vis-à-vis their community or society as a whole?

Of course a manager should always behave in an exemplary manner. But his role in heading up a company is above all to allow his collaborators to develop their own responsibilities. The company's culture should allow individual initiative to thrive, in the interest of the company but also for the good of everyone. How? This is emphatically not a question of regulations. Strict attention to honesty and to the basic principles of community is essential, but the environment you create is the real key. Benetton is lucky in that we are present in more than one hundred countries around the world, which has taught us to listen to and understand different cultures.

What concrete changes has the emergence of Corporate Responsibility brought about in your company? And what further changes are to come?

I could list for you all the regulatory initiatives taken in recent years, in particular with the Sarbanes-Oxley law. But I would rather use an example to better illustrate management's sense of corporate responsibility. Our headquarters was once a factory. A purely economic approach would have dictated that this location be destroyed and a new one built in its place. But these buildings are loaded with history. We chose to renovate them with the help of respected architects, which meant that the work took much longer and cost a great deal more. I believe this decision was worth it, as we succeeded in creating a remarkable work space which nurtures our employees' creativity, though I'm not sure our investors feel the same way.
The responsibility of the head of a company, in this case a large publicly-owned company, lies here, in the ability to reconcile apparently divergent interests. Shareholders have perfectly legitimate concerns as the owners of the company. They entrust me, the head of the company, with the job of increasing the value of their investment. At the same time, we know that fund managers favour a fairly rapid return on their investments. Once again, traders are legitimate purveyors of the liquidities which markets need. But I cannot always

satisfy their expectations in the short term. As I have explained, I may even take decisions which are against their interests in the short term. If I say this publicly, tomorrow my stock loses 10% of its value. But my responsibility as a manager, towards society, towards my employees, and also towards my shareholders, is to know when to resist short-term pressures which are not good for the company.

In the medium and long term, however, I am convinced that everyone's interests come together. Only time will reduce these apparent differences. What is needed in these cases, with regard to the stock market, is transparency and a willingness to explain one's choices.

How are these changes beneficial to today's companies?

I believe these changes will be beneficial to companies, and I think this attitude is more and more prevalent. Companies adapt on their own, because it is in their interest. I am a strong believer in the choices and pressures applied by consumers. When consumers decide to favor products from companies which protect the environment and which are socially responsible and transparent in their operations, everyone will join in. There is already a trend in this direction, though it is still in the minority. But I believe in positive reinforcement: if consumers demand responsible behavior, companies will become more responsible, will communicate on the subject and raise consumer consciousness. In this way, best practices will evolve into norms.

Ethical funds will evolve in the same way. When they perform as well, or almost, as other funds, I am certain that investors will flock towards them – which will encourage companies to make even more efforts. In the two cases I mention here, there would be a financial advantage for the company in acting responsibly. Today, responsibility is still most often at a cost.

How would you rate the public image of companies and CEOs in today's society?

As far as Benetton is concerned, we are lucky to have a positive image – and perhaps we influence this "luck." In general, Italians tend to have a positive opinion of managers of prominent companies, some of whom, such as Olivetti during the post-WWII reconstruction phase, truly influenced their generation. This is even sometimes apparent in their political voting intentions. That said, the mediocre performance of the economy in recent years has negatively affected companies' images. Relocations and unemployment have tarnished the images of companies, on which there is a tendency to place the blame.

Martin Bouygues
Chairman and CEO of Bouygues group

"Strong personal commitment."

To whom and how are today's companies accountable?

I will remain true to my business philosophy and my "trilogy". A company is first of all accountable to its clients, then to its employees, and finally to its shareholders. With current social trends, companies have also become accountable to the environment in which they evolve: this is what is known as Sustainable Development, with the notion of "environment" defined in very broad terms.

This commitment is very concrete at Bouygues, and I participate personally by attending training courses in ethics, respect and company performance. We recently held our 31st such seminar, during which, as for those preceding, I was the speaker for a half-day session. I would add that not a week goes by when I don't meet with Group employees from our various businesses and with different levels of responsibility. These meetings usually involve between 20 and 400 people, and constitute real opportunities for dialogue.

In seventeen years as Chairman, I have thus met tens of thousands of employees. Most of the discussions I have with them concern our corporate philosophy, our culture, our role in society, our responsibilities and our development. I regularly ask them: "What is our company's purpose?" They comment and I also give them my answer: "To serve our clients." This requires, at least for long-term performance, surrounding ourselves with efficient, motivated and ethical employees, because, to come back to the "trilogy" mentioned above, if we serve our clients to the best of our ability thanks to the quality of our teams, then our shareholders will be satisfied.

It is by staying true to these principles that we have, over the past fifteen years, achieved considerable progress, without however communicating about it outside the company. I make it a principle to prove everything I say.

As the top manager of a major corporation, how do you personally experience this responsibility?

It is a constant commitment; sometimes a heavy load, as it includes numerous facets. I carry, first of all, the responsibility of defining our corporate culture and communicating it as broadly as possible. Clearly, this is not a purely individual exercise. I work in close cooperation with my senior executives. I am also the spokesperson who must ensure that our actions are in concert with the values and principles which we promote. In this perspective, each word used is of capital importance. Our language must faithfully reflect our corporate culture in a context in which the pursuit of transparency (and thus democracy) is very strong.

It seems perfectly natural to me to be personally involved in this process. I do so with great pleasure, as did my father before me (editor's note: Francis Bouygues).

Do you believe today's top executives have to lead by example, vis-à-vis their employees and vis-à-vis their community or society as a whole?

Of course, example is everything. If my actions don't conform to my words, then my leadership is no longer credible. This principle is without exception, and is thus an inflexible rule. If I can allow myself a brief digression, we can probably observe here one explanation of the split between political and economic affairs which is so palpable in a country like France. The demands made of each sphere are not the same.

The accountability of managers and of companies has been affected by three remarkable catalysts over the past fifty years. The first was the consumer movement, which came from the United States and modified the relationship between companies and their clients, with the latter becoming increasingly demanding. Next came the workers' rights movement, and the development of labor legislation and case law, which govern relations between companies and their employees. Today's framework is significantly more protective than in the previous era. Finally, the relationship between corporate executives and their shareholders has been modernized. These changes have codified corporate management and increased organizational transparency. The company that cheats today is denounced and sanctioned fairly quickly. Which is normal. We have seen a true revolution in this area since the end of World War II. Is there evidence of a similar trend in the political sphere? It would be interesting to go into the matter in more detail.

What concrete changes has the emergence of Corporate Responsibility brought about in your company? And what further changes are to come?

The complete reorganization of our subsidiaries' boards of directors through the various committees which I initiated (accounts, ethics and sponsorship, selection of directors, etc.) is a concrete example of changes which have taken place in recent years. I apply this management system with equal strictness to both our listed and unlisted subsidiaries.

At the Group level, and within each business, a Sustainable Development Department has been created, which plays a role of agitator and think-tank.

We have made progress and will continue to do so, but for this we must come up with arguments, educate, share our convictions and have an unshakable will to honor our commitments. Sustainable development at Bouygues is a little like the writings of Molière's character, Monsieur Jourdain: we have always done it without calling it so. These past years, we have begun to structure our sustainable development policy in order to report on it.

Among the concrete actions we have implemented, we could mention our sponsorship initiatives, which essentially address humanitarian and equal-opportunity issues. It is in this spirit that we recently created the Francis Bouygues Foundation, whose objective is to help those who, for financial reasons, have difficulty pursuing their chosen area of study. Concretely, we assist young people who have graduated with honors from their secondary-school studies and who are in financial difficulty. We support them for four to six years, as everyone knows that the first years of study, particularly programs to prepare for entrance into major business and engineering schools, require an enormous amount of work. It is impossible to pass entrance exams when also working in a multitude of part-time jobs. When we reach "cruising speed", we should be assisting between 300 and 350 students at any given time. When a Group like ours has the means to take on a project such as this one, we consider it a normal thing to do. It is part of our role.

In addition, I think these are healthy initiatives. Formerly, all redistribution of wealth took place at State level through taxes on citizens and companies. Today, companies can directly take on a portion of this redistribution. We can see exactly where the money goes, and in the end this is very empowering for the company and its employees. I would add that our shareholders support this project and have thus shown enormous generosity.

How are these changes beneficial to today's companies?

My entire corporate philosophy is based on one simple idea: the only reason we exist is to serve and defend the interests of our clients. If we follow this principle, we will necessarily derive benefit. I created Maison Bouygues catalogue homes in 1979 with this philosophy, and it allowed us to become number two in the market in just a few years. We built some 40,000 family homes and we never had a major conflict with any client. I created Bouygues Telecom in the same spirit. Today, all the companies in the Group are on board and know that we profit or will profit in a way which is difficult to quantify but very real. If we get up in the morning with the sole idea of becoming richer, we may earn money, but not in the long term.

However, if we get up with the desire to work better each day than the one before and better than our competitors, we have a good chance of creating lasting wealth. In the end, it is encouraging to know that by working well and respecting our values, we have every chance of moving the company forward.

How would you rate the public image of companies and CEOs in today's society?

France is an old country with a traditional political ideology in which profit is suspect. In fact, we are one of the only countries in the world for which this is true. Still, there is no doubt that the image of French companies is improving even if a few lame ducks, whether individuals or companies, sometimes sully management image. But I am one of those who believe that truth will triumph in the end.

Particularly because in a world which is destabilized by rapid change, economic and corporate realities provide real reference points. In fact, I am struck by a growing gap between the situation of individuals within a company and their situation in society. In the former, people are asked to take on more and more responsibility; in the latter, less and less. At times, in fact, society acts as a protective cocoon in which people need not take responsibility for their actions. From this perspective, companies play a very positive role in transmitting the values of accountability.

Henri de Castries
Chairman of the Board of AXA

"A real potential to be vectors for progress."

To whom and how are today's companies accountable?

A company is a community of men and women who have chosen to join a common economic project. By responding appropriately and efficiently to its clients' needs, a company creates wealth for its employees, as well as for the shareholders who support its activity. The payment of wages and dividends represents the company's core responsibility.

This core is being progressively extended as new ambitions and needs emerge within the company itself and in the economic and social environment. Let us take an example. Employees are increasingly expected to show flexibility and the ability to evolve. A company is responsible for contributing to the improvement of these skills. AXA helps its employees develop their qualifications in a working environment which we consider to be both empowering and respectful of the individual. This is a win-win process: it benefits each employee, and also supports the performance of the company as a whole.

A company's responsibilities do not, today, end at its door. They have expanded in response to the demands of a diversified network of stakeholders: consumers, public opinion, suppliers, media, associations, NGOs... and this, for a group such as AXA, in a wide variety of national contexts.

Moreover, large international groups such as ours are frequently seen as jointly responsible (with national governments) for harmonious global development. These companies are creators of wealth and under constant pressure to evolve and adapt, and as such have a very real potential to be vectors of progress. Therefore, in terms of economic performance and management quality, they carry a heavy responsibility. Oversight committees, management boards and financial markets are quick to remind them of this when necessary. However, national governments are in most cases more apt to create legislative restraints than to support true globalization of trade, education and economies.

Companies thus find themselves facing complex and sometimes contradictory expectations. These expectations are not necessarily perceived as constraints, however. AXA is naturally interested in societal expectations, starting – for obvious reasons of legitimacy and know-how – with those which relate to its profession and its clients: risk prevention, education, social exclusion. We express our culture of corporate responsibility in particular through charitable undertakings. Allow me to mention the one which, to me, best expresses the quality of the community of men and women which I describe above. AXA Hearts in Action was created 15 years ago and is a social philanthropy program. Some 15,000 AXA employees worldwide contribute their expertise, their time and their generosity in support to the disadvantaged, the disabled and others who are marginalized.

Companies must also accept their responsibility as "living entities," and the impact of their activity on the environment. The *direct* responsibility of a leader in the Financial Protection sector is clearly less than that of a large industrial group. However, this is still not a minor issue for AXA because of the role we can play as insurer and investor. The considerable volumes of capital we manage confer us a responsibility which we are willing to assume. This is one of the reasons of our support to the Carbon Disclosure Project, which allows important investors to better evaluate carbon-emissions risks.

As the top manager of a major corporation, how do you personally experience this responsibility?

My mission is to pass on the company I manage to the next generation in the best possible conditions.
This mission requires that:
  – I continue to surround myself with men and women whose skills and values allow them to meet competitive challenges, and at the same time provide all our team members with a professional environment in which they can carry out their potential;
  – I consolidate a corporate vision and culture which allow our clients and society in general to receive the benefits of our profession;
  – I confirm AXA's position as a leader in Financial Protection to the benefit of its partners.

In short, it is an exciting and inspiring responsibility, which I intend to exercise with both serenity and determination.

Do you believe today's top-executives have to lead by example vis-a-vis their employees and vis-a-vis their community or society as a whole?

"It is not the path that is difficult, but that which is difficult which is the path." This quote from the philosopher Simone Weil seems to set an unreachable standard at first sight. It is nonetheless an excellent reference for those who must, as managers, meet enormous challenges. Progressively transforming this standard into a necessity, before making it a way of life, greatly helps in taking on the responsibility of setting an example which you describe.

Because my job involves, to a great extent, defining, communicating and guiding AXA's business strategy, my personal behaviour – like that of every member of the Executive Committee – must also represent and support AXA's values: teamwork, keeping promises, innovation, realism and professionalism.

However, if the Executive Committee were to take on this role alone, it would have quite a limited domino effect. Each of our managers must have the will and courage to lead actions according to what they expect from their co-workers. The "I say what I do" becomes indivisible from the "I do what I say" This is necessary regards to our collaborators but also in relation to our other stakeholders.

What concrete changes has the emergence of Corporate Responsibility brought about in your company? And what further changes are to come?

AXA strongly believes that a company can achieve sustainable development only through involvement in the society in which it carries out its business. In 2003, we formally defined our commitments to our most important partners, and defined a sustainable development strategy which we are now implementing step by step.

As in any other function of a company we must measure our actions in order to allow progress. That is why, in order to receive an external assessment of our engagement, we solicited a corporate responsibility evaluation from Vigeo, an independent agency specialized in this field, at the end of 2004.

Six areas were analyzed: human rights, human resources, customer and supplier relations, environment, societal engagement and corporate governance. The resulting evaluation – a diagnosis of the Group's policies, tools and results in terms of responsibility – allowed us to identify our strengths and weaknesses and to further specify our priorities.

AXA's sustainable development strategy is defined around two poles. The first aims at comforting our corporate responsibility. In the area of human resources, we support the professional development of our employees, and stress diversity and gender equality. In regards to our commitment to civil society, AXA will develop programs which give priority to prevention and social philanthropy through its involvement in AXA Hearts in Action. In the environmental area programs for reducing paper and energy consumption will be implemented, and AXA locations will progressively adopt HQE (High Environmental Quality) standards (as defined by the French legislation). Finally, when selecting suppliers, we will evaluate their commitment to sustainable development and require that Human Rights issues be mentioned in the contracts

The second pole aims at setting sustainable development at the heart of AXA's activity, because the best way the Group can contribute to economic and social development is by carrying out its business in a responsible manner. In general insurance AXA's priority is risk prevention through actions which limit the number of accidents, and the development of research on emerging risks to create new products. In the field of life insurance, AXA intends to offer pension plans which are more productive and flexible. In the asset management field, governance will be reinforced, through active voting in the general assembly as well as transparency of information on the funds in which our clients invest.

Finally, a word about the future: We want AXA to become the preferred company in the Financial Protection sector. I have the conviction that, in regards to the stakeholder's new expectations, we can achieve that goal only by becoming the global society's preferred company. One of the necessary conditions for this is that AXA fully accepts its social responsibilities through concrete commitments in terms of sustainable development.

How are these changes beneficial to today's companies?

I would be tempted to answer that my only certitude concerns the additional costs induced by any new constraint on the short term.

However, good management of these new socio-economic issues may, in the longer term, allow companies to have more efficient relations with certain stakeholders. We cannot therefore yet measure the supposed positive impact, but I can attempt to illustrate its nature.

Financially, some analysts believe that companies which are well-regarded in terms of environmental and social criteria may, in the long run, be able to achieve profitability that is higher than the market average thanks to better risk management. As specialists in risk management, and as investors, we are obviously sensitive to this line of thought.

In terms of business, approaching this topic together should allow us to be always more in sync with society's expectations, and thereby closer to our clients.

How would you rate the public image of companies and CEOs in today's society?

French public opinion remains fairly wary, if not mistrustful, of companies in general and top executives in particular. In contrast, internal surveys of employees show – as in AXA's case – a generally favourable attitude towards their own company.

Despite certain laudable but still isolated efforts, politicians and the media contribute only marginally to bridging the gap between these two perspectives. They do not favour the emergence of an entrepreneurial culture enough, however important it may be in a country often accused by external observers of lacking ambition and dynamism.

Nonetheless one cannot give into pessimism or simply accept the sterile observation. While companies must continue to focus primarily on their own activity and the economic development which it induces, they must also participate in certain Global Society debates. This is precisely what AXA does on a regular basis. Thereby the company proves that profit is not its only area of interest and shows public opinion that the corporate world is also capable of having a soul.

Adi Godrej
Chairman and CEO of the Godrej Group

"Good governance is the top priority."

To whom and how are today's companies accountable?

Companies today are accountable primarily to their shareholders, but also significantly to their employees, their customers, their suppliers, their other business relations and of course, the environment in which they operate.

One is often given the impression that serving all of these stakeholders can lead to trade-offs. But in today's environment, a number of companies have found that being on good terms with all of their stakeholders has improved their position. Companies that can show that they are socially responsible can, over the long haul, gain recognition and a favourable reputation – what economists call "reputation capital". A good reputation can lead to all kinds of benefits such as better relations with employees, easier access to credit, and customer and supplier loyalty. Investors are more willing to trust their investments to firms that have better reputations because they perceive fewer risks. And indeed, there is even evidence showing a correlation between corporate social performance and long-term profitability

As the top manager of a major corporation, how do you personally live this responsibility?

The Godrej Group has completed 109 years and enjoys one of the strongest reputations of trust with the Indian consumer. We have had a tradition of category-defining products, a strong employee culture and a distinct emphasis on giving back to society in various fields.

I consider, as Chairman of the Group, my main responsibilities revolve around Corporate Governance, Human Resource Development, Performance Orientation and Corporate Social Responsibility.

Do you believe today's top-executives have to lead by example vis-a-vis their employees and vis-a-vis their community or society as a whole?

I believe a very large number of corporations and executives today are becoming increasingly aware and conscious of their social responsibilities. This is being seen both at the organizational level and at an individual level. I believe that there are several global and Indian Corporate leaders who display these trends in an exemplary manner. Globally, Shell has been doing an exemplary job in the areas of environmental responsibility and the quest for renewable sources of energy. In our own way, we are working with the Indian farming community through "Aadhar" – our rural retailing initiative – in terms of working with them on improving productivity, involvement with initiatives on social development and improving general standards of living.

What are the main tangible changes the emergence of Corporate Responsibility has brought up in the working of your company? And what do you believe are the main changes to come?

The emergence of Corporate Responsibility has brought a greater focus on value creation in all of group companies. A few years ago, we introduced EVA – Economic Value Added – as the principal financial metric for the Group. EVA is the residual profits after the cost of capital used has been deducted. A large number of our employees are on a performance-linked variable remuneration system which is linked to EVA improvement in the business.

We have introduced a strong performance management system. We force-rank all our managers. We reward top-performers disproportionately and put the laggards under the scanner. The best talent in the group is identified through a structured process and mentored carefully. Rewards and recognition are used to spur both individual and team performance. There is a very strong emphasis on performance which needs to be attained within the framework of out cherished values.

The other important dimension of corporate responsibility is the Board of Directors. An alert and well-governing Board inhibits conflict of interest between accountants, lawyers, analysts, investment bankers, and consultants; ensures the presence of strong internal controls and a commitment to compliance; and confirms third-party verification. The Godrej Group is a mainly private group, so I will indicate what we do for corporate governance from the Board's point of view in our flagship publicly listed company, Godrej Consumer Products Ltd. GCPL has a strong Board. Half the Board members are independent directors, who are professionals of distinction in their respective fields. These independent directors are well compensated by Indian standards and are expected to spend quality time with the company. The Board inspires and ensures strong corporate governance, strategic posture and performance orientation in the company.

How are these changes beneficial to today's companies?

Good governance provides a competitive advantage in the global marketplace. Well governed companies raise capital widely, easily, and cheaply. Good governance also leads to improved employee morale and higher productivity. Another well researched fact is that well-governed companies last longer and have a far better record at creating long-term shareholder value.

How would you rate the public image of companies and CEOs in today's society?

Globally, the public image of corporations took a beating post-Enron and other such scams. I feel there is a considerable improvement in the last year or so. In India, the public image of business is at an all time high and getting better.

Stephen Green
Chairman and Executive Director of the HSBC Group

"Exemplary behaviour in all business dealings."

To whom and how are today's companies accountable?

Companies are responsible to their clients, their shareholders, their employees and also to the communities in which they operate. I don't believe that this responsibility has changed, or that it is more a feature of our times than of any time in the past. What has changed, however, is the expression, by the parties involved themselves, of what they expect from companies in terms of responsibility. For some years now, this new source of pressure has led a growing number of companies to formalise their policies in this area, often basing the process on their core values.

We believe that the prime responsibility of a company is to perform well. For a group like HSBC, the main aim is to produce a satisfactory return for investors. We are also well aware that our commercial responsibilities go hand in hand with our social obligations. HSBC Holdings plc is one of the world's leading banking and financial services groups and, as a result, makes a significant contribution to social and economic development around the globe. Our responsibility is to support this development, whilst ensuring, as far as possible, that it will not have a negative environmental, economic or social impact in the short, medium or long term.

This is why we seek to conduct our business in a way that meets the highest standards of professionalism and integrity and why we are determined to play our full role in the communities we serve.

**As a senior manager of a major company,
how do you personally experience this responsibility?**

I am very proud to lead the HSBC Group. One of the reasons for this is the fact that my personal values are very similar to those of the company. I know that this sense of shared values makes a strong contribution to the pride that so many of my fellow employees take in belonging to our group.

I believe that these values of responsibility are intrinsic to our group, to our brand. Whatever our role within the company, it is our duty to build on, apply and transmit these values. This is how we will ensure the continued success of our company. It is also by recognising that these values are not just for the group's managers but that all staff breathe life into them through their work from day to day, for as long as they are part of the group.

Do you believe today's top-executives have to lead by example vis-a-vis their employees and vis-a-vis their community or society as a whole?

The HSBC Group has more than 280,000 employees around the world and it is clear that anyone who leads such a company must ensure exemplary behaviour in all business dealings. This is also essential to safeguard the group's reputation. Long-term success is built on confidence, mutual respect and shared goals.

As far as setting an example to society is concerned, I believe that all employees have a responsibility to behave in an exemplary fashion. Of course managers are the most visible, but failings anywhere in the organisation will be visible to all areas of society, irrespective of where in the company they occur.

Just as we all need to take responsibility, we all need to set a good example.

What concrete changes has the increased focus on the notion of responsibility brought in your company? What changes do you expect to see in future?

Above all, we have structured our businesses so as to make it easier to integrate responsibility at all levels of the company. We have created a CSR Committee of the Group's Board of Directors, to supervise the implementation of the Group's social and environmental responsibility policies and to advise the Board, its committees and individual executives. The CSR Executive Steering Group monitors the implementation of the various concrete measures being introduced. Lastly, we have created a new unit, the Sustainable Development Group, which will seek to ensure that the principle of sustainability is better integrated into HSBC's businesses, both in terms of opportunities and risks.

This approach has enabled the definition and implementation of a risk management policy that includes social and environmental criteria when we are considering the financing of a project. This includes the adoption of and compliance with the Equator Principles[1]. It has also led to the creation and introduction of sector-specific guidelines, setting out the international standards to be followed when we lend to or invest in companies or projects in high-risk sectors.

As another example, we have introduced a global programme to reduce our direct impact on the environment, and committed ourselves to be carbon neutral. We are building awareness of the issues amongst all our staff and encouraging them to reduce their consumption of energy, paper, water and travel. Consumption in all these areas, and the improvements we are making around the world, are monitored and measured. The results are collated at our head office. We have undertaken to offset the emissions we cause by investing in carbon credit projects.

What benefits have these changes brought to your company?

Sustainability matters because the societies in which we operate tell us it matters. We believe it complements profit, and for this reason, sustainability is part of our growth strategy and our brand.

What sort of image do you think society has of business and business leaders?

Business has different images globally and locally and these change over time.

At the moment, in emerging economies, businesses are seen as opportunities for growth and greater openness. At the same time, the image of business has been adversely affected by various well-known scandals in recent years. Bad news tends to grab the headlines, whereas good news does not always get the coverage it should. As a result, I think that the image of business and of business leaders is quite fragile in our fast-changing world. We all need to adjust and adapt to help build confidence and continue to drive progress in the right direction.

---

1. HSBC adopted the Equator Principles in 2003 and has joined other large institutions for the launch of the revised Equator Principles, which constitute a framework for social and environmental risk management related to project finance. This new version is the fruit of the experience of 40 financial institutions from around the world which currently apply these Principles.

Daniel Janssen
Chairman of the Board of Directors of Solvay
(until May 2006)

"Help people solve their problems beyond purely economic issues."

To whom and how are today's companies accountable?

Legally, the Board of Directors is accountable to shareholders, but a company is accountable to its stakeholders, which are its shareholders, employees, clients and all groups affected directly or indirectly by the company's business. Solvay has 400 locations around the world. In many cases, these are chemical plants in sparsely populated areas or near villages. When we arrive, we frequently build roads, houses, schools and, when necessary, for example, we test the quality of the local water supply before settling in. When we announce our intentions in some countries, there is a reaction of surprise. But Solvay's 143 years of history illustrate a constant concern for our environment, and we are perceived as credible in this role. For example, we own a PVC-production plant in Thailand. One day the King of Thailand, who knew of our local initiatives, asked to meet with me. During the interview, he spoke almost exclusively of the environment and finally asked if Solvay could help with cleaning up a nearby canal, which we did. I could cite numerous other examples to illustrate this responsibility. We do have an obligation to help people solve their problems, beyond purely economic questions.

What is a company responsible for? Solvay is responsible for carrying out its mission. This sentence is written into our annual report. And we define our mission very broadly; it naturally includes the economic and financial spheres, but also carries social and environmental meanings. We work to achieve our objectives in all these areas.

As the top manager of a major corporation, how do you personally experience this responsibility?

I approach this responsibility with pride and dedication, and also with the goal of effective action. My responsibility, along with that of the other senior executives, is to bring about sustainable and profitable development for the company. Allow me a brief foray into our history to help you better understand my meaning. Solvay was founded in 1863 by my ancestor Ernest Solvay, who was 25 years old at the time and had already twice failed at other undertakings, and his 23-year-old brother. And in twenty years, they developed what was perhaps the first truly multinational company in the world. Their parents, from the small business sphere, were very strict people with a strong sense of morals. Ernest Solvay himself was passionate about the social responsibilities of entrepreneurs and companies. Thus, in 1905, he offered health insurance, paid vacation and retirement pensions to his employees – not just Solvay's Belgian workers, but all the company's employees around the world. And remember, Belgium's social security system was created only in 1947. Education was another passion, and he created the Solvay Institute of Physics and Chemistry and a School of Business, as well as providing significant financing to the University of Brussels. He was co-opted as a senator by the liberal camp – in the American sense of the word, that is, left of centre politically. His mark on the company's history and on his successors remains very strong. As a member of the fifth generation, I have always strived to keep the word "ethics" associated with the Solvay name.
I believe that a president is not only the leader of his company, but is also a leadership figure in an evolving society. We are influential citizens. We must accept this responsibility, even if the process takes time. This belief explains my longstanding activism within Belgian and European business circles and my support for European construction, as well as my interest in education. The latter has been expressed most recently in the 2004 creation of the "Corporate Social Responsibility" Chair which carries my name at the Solvay School of Business.

Do you believe today's top-executives have to lead by example vis-a-vis their employees and vis-a-vis their community or society as a whole?

Clearly yes, and not only the president, but management in a broader sense: directors of subsidiaries, national executives and all of upper-level management must be models of good practices. Each person must promote the values in which he or she believes. About fifteen years ago, we surveyed Solvay's managers to find out what had motivated their decision to join the firm. The idea of "ethics" stood out as the top criterion of choice. We were very proud of this because these are the values which guarantee the permanence of a company. Further, the company itself should be a role model. Stakeholders should be aware that Solvay takes care of its surrounding environment. We believe this to be the case. I know that the general public is suspicious of such statements and believes them to be a mere façade, doubtless because companies have stressed "shareholder value" to the detriment of "stakeholder value" over the past twenty years. The former is essential, but it is not enough.

Finally, I would like to add that family shareholders in a large company also carry a great responsibility towards society, which explains the political engagement of many members of my own family.

What concrete changes has the emergence of Corporate Responsibility brought about in your company? And what further changes are to come?

As I mentioned, Solvay has been practicing social responsibility for 143 years. However, the form our engagement takes has changed over time and with the growth of the company. Our value system and our priorities have evolved. At the end of the 19th century, issues of famine and of the education of our employees were dominant. Today, and doubtless for the next ten or twenty years, the two major challenges confronting us are environmental pollution and social inequality, particularly in the developing world. Humanity faces here very real challenges.

Solvay has also evolved from an operational perspective. Twenty years ago, when we began developing our activity in Asia, we felt the need to create a written code of ethics, which had been implicit until that time. Certain people within the organization questioned the necessity of drafting a document which in some companies remains only tacit. But for Solvay, this is not a purely formal document or a marketing ploy. In fact, we do not communicate it outside of the company; it is our own business. This code sets very concrete rules for our teams in each country. Every two to five years, the Executive Committee adapts it to the changing environment. At the same time, ethics are a subject of daily debate within the company. These debates often relate to very complex questions in situations which are rarely black and white; instead, they require constant arbitration.

Finally, a word on Solvay's involvement, as an industry, in global warming. We have made enormous efforts in the past twenty years to reduce our CO_2 emissions. We were producing fluoride gases without being aware, for many years, of their destructive effect on the ozone layer. We offered to eliminate them on our own, announcing our intentions to the UN and providing a schedule for action, and we allotted significant sums to research for the development of replacement products. Every company has a sector of more or less importance in which it can make a difference.

How are these changes beneficial to today's companies?

I am convinced that respect for social responsibility helps to ensure a company's long-term development. Solvay has survived three wars, the emergence of Nazism in Germany, and the communist revolution in Russia, where we had a strong presence. These events led to the destruction of over half of the company's assets. But we always bounced back, thanks, I believe, to our attitude and to the values we adhere to; thanks also to the loyalty of the Belgian population, which supports these same values. Our attachment to Belgium is strong. We have always chosen to be involved in the country's development, and I think the Belgians have in return shown their attachment to our company.

An anecdote, if you permit, will illustrate the importance of ethics and the way in which they mould a company's image. In 1939, the director of a factory we owned in Cracow, Poland, asked the Executive Committee in Brussels for permission to hire a score of young local Resistance fighters in order to protect them from Nazi persecution. Management at that time accepted. It happens that among these youths was a certain Karol Wojtyla, the future Pope Jean-Paul II, who thus worked for Solvay for several years. Knowledge of this story spread, and after the collapse of the Iron Curtain in 1989, Lech Walesa, who was not yet President at the time, invited me to Poland to tell me he would be glad if Solvay would take back its factories which had been confiscated by the communist regime.

While an ethical approach and social responsibility may have a cost in the short term, I am persuaded that they are frequently profitable in the long term. This is also why a family firm is perhaps more sensitive to these questions. We want to be around in another 143 years.

How would you rate the public image of companies and CEOs in today's society?

Let us be frank. Executives of large companies today are generally perceived as efficient and competent, but also self-interested and ungenerous. However, I think that people who form this opinion are underestimating something of which they lack knowledge.
Many executives, in top management and also at other levels, are incredibly generous and not at all self-interested. They do their job and they do it with respect for the common interest. But it is true that capitalism is too often marked by its dark and greedy side.

Martin Roman
Chairman and CEO of ČEZ

"Strive to earn the trust of all our stakeholders."

To whom and how are today's companies accountable?

The primary accountability of companies is to their owners. At present, all companies operate in a network of interlinked relations and therefore also have to respect rightful interests of other stakeholders – employees, customers and communities. If a company strives for long-term success, it has always to try to make others understand and trust its business.

**As the top manager of a major corporation,
how do you personally experience this responsibility?**

Increasing the value of ČEZ is my primary concern in making any decision. For example, we do not invest abroad in order to control a larger corporation. We purchase assets only if they add value to this company – it is not by coincidence that the ČEZ stock began to grow after we refused to outbid Slovak power companies during privatization. I personally put great emphasis on communication with stakeholders through the media and through many direct contacts.

**Do you believe today's top-executives have to lead by example
vis-a-vis their employees and vis-a-vis their community
or society as a whole?**

Of course. In an environment where your every statement or action may provoke the reaction of thousands of people on the Internet, one does not have the liberty of saying one thing and doing another.

What concrete changes has the emergence of Corporate Responsibility brought about in your company? And what further changes are to come?

In recent years, ČEZ has become by far the most generous donor in the Czech Republic. Our foundation supports hundreds of projects focused on childhood development, culture and sports. We look for other ways of improving the quality of life in the vicinity of our power stations, and of working with local communities.
Stakeholders' opinions are taken into account when we make business decisions. For example, we have started to support recoverable energy resources more actively. We also try to act in the right way in ordinary everyday activities – we adjust high-voltage lines so they do not pose a threat for birds, to cite an example.

How are these changes beneficial to today's companies?

I see the main benefit of these changes in the fact that they make companies look to the future, which is always for their good.

How would you rate the public image of companies and CEOs in today's society?

It is a bit harder for us in Central Europe than for our Anglo-Saxon colleagues. Success is not admired, but rather viewed with suspicion here. That is why the present global wave of distrust of big corporations makes no substantial difference for us.

Arun Sarin
CEO of Vodafone

"Conducting all aspects of our business ethically and being open about how we operate."

To whom and how are today's companies accountable?

Today's companies, in addition to their shareholders, customers and employees, are accountable to a range of other stakeholders who are affected in one way or another by their actions. Organisations, particularly large organisations with influence, are expected to address the challenges presented by their impact on society both at a macro and micro level.

For example the mobile sector has a responsibility to ensure that people are comfortable with the placement of masts in local communities and, on a wider level, they have to account for the way in which their technology has changed society whether this is from a positive perspective, by empowering individuals through providing access to communications, or from a negative perspective, by considering issues such as privacy, child protection or health.

As the top-manager of a major corporation, how do you personally live this responsibility?

My vision for the Vodafone corporate responsibility programme is that ultimately it will become fully integrated into everything we do – in fact it will be instinctive. I aim to achieve this by embedding corporate responsibility into the organisation's values and strategy. We have gone some way to achieve this by identifying four core values, one of which is a "passion for the world around us" and we have included being a responsible business as one of our six strategic goals. This means that I, alongside everyone else within the organisation, have become truly accountable for our actions from a corporate responsibility perspective and will be personally judged on this as we carry out our daily work.

Do you believe today's top-executives have to lead by example vis-a-vis their employees and vis-a-vis their community or society as a whole?

Yes. If you want employees to take their responsibilities seriously, it is important that top executives lead by example. I am proud of the CR initiatives our business has implemented over the last year and am delighted to have the opportunity to share them with our staff and other stakeholder groups. Take, for example, the recent SIM (Socio-economic Impact of Mobiles) report on the impact that mobile phones have had in Africa. The findings from the report taught us a great deal – primarily around the ways in which mobiles are used in the developing world. It is wrong to simply extrapolate our developed world models of needs and usage patterns to developing nations. Understanding context is vital and we hope that the studies we have published will assist in highlighting the role that mobile telecommunications can play to encourage sustainable development.

What are the main tangible changes the emergence of Corporate Responsibility has brought up in the working of your company? And what do you believe are the main changes to come?

The creation of a corporate responsibility team has enabled us to better organise ourselves to identify and manage areas of concern on a proactive basis. It also allows us to focus on products and services which have a "social" benefit as well as a commercial benefit.
In addition, developing targets and ensuring compliance through a public audit helps to generate and sustain trust and confidence amongst staff and shareholders alike. This, of course, is key to the success of any organisation.

How are these changes beneficial to today's companies?

The changes are beneficial in a variety of ways. It makes good financial sense for example to reduce the amount of energy we use. We do this in a number of ways, for example by using renewable energy in some instances and ensuring that our technical equipment is recycled or reused. We have also undertaken a number of other cost-saving initiatives such as partnering with equipment manufacturers and working with them to assess the energy performance of their current products and discussing plans for introducing more energy efficient equipment.
However corporate responsibility is not just about our approach to social and environmental issues. It implies conducting all aspects of

our business ethically and being open about how we operate. This includes areas like supply chain management, financial management and political engagement. The success and rigour of these processes has a significant influence on consumer and investor confidence which has a direct impact on our sales and share price.

How would you rate the public image of companies and CEOs in today's society?

It is no secret that the level of trust in multinational companies has decreased during the last 10 years. As CEO of one of the world's largest organisations I believe we at Vodafone have a responsibility to address this. In a world where billions of people live in poverty, where the population continues to grow and where the earth resources are being over-exploited, we cannot afford to let things take their course. At Vodafone we believe it is possible to meet the challenges presented by the responsible delivery of products and services, on all levels, and ensure that our customers, stakeholders and investors have the confidence to work with us to achieve sustainable business models for the future.

Ernest-Antoine Seillière
President of the Supervisory Board
of Wendel Investissement

"Commitment and responsibility belong to society as a whole."

To whom and how are today's companies accountable?

I am curious about the way you have formulated your question and about the meaning which you give to the term "accountability." In fact, it is society as a whole which invests companies with the mission of satisfying a certain number of fundamental individual and collective needs, in particular the creation of wealth and jobs. Commitment and responsibility belong, therefore, to society as a whole. By limiting discussion to corporate accountability, we imply that accountability is one-way, and even introduce an accusatory note, the insinuation being that only companies must be held accountable. Again, companies act and develop at the behest of and in the interest of society in general. Therefore, I think it is more appropriate to ask ourselves: with whom companies must work together today? The response is contained in the question itself: with all members of society. A true awakening is needed in this area. The battle for employment and growth is a collective responsibility.

Using this joint commitment as a starting point, there are a certain number of consequences for companies, because their activity does have direct and indirect effects on their entire human, economic and social environments. Companies thus clearly have particular responsibility towards those who are involved in the production process; that is, the shareholders and the employees. Next, towards their clients. And finally, vis-à-vis society in general, particularly in matters of education and environmental protection.

As the top manager of a major corporation,
how do you personally experience this responsibility?

Wendel Investissement has a very specific profile owing to our strong historical ties and family roots. The Group celebrated its 300th anniversary in 2004 and has always been under family control. I belong to the ninth generation of managers. This history leads managers of the company to give priority to long-term development. Principles of continuity and responsibility guide our actions. At the same time, the group's culture lends great importance to the individual within the company. For a long time, the history of the Wendel family was linked to a single economic sector, steelmaking, and a single region, the Lorraine. This model proved to be extremely solid. There was real solidarity between the company and the society in which it evolved. The interdependency was evident in so-called "social paternalism." The company contributed to the development of local housing, health care, education etc. This system has of course disappeared, but the importance of the human factor remains. It is expressed in a strong vision of delegated responsibility within the company, and a management approach based on trust and on direct relationships in which the individual is at the centre of activity.

Do you believe today's top-executives have to lead by example
vis-a-vis their employees and vis-a-vis their community
or society as a whole?

Corporate executives must be role models for society, but to accomplish this they must first accept their own visibility and not be afraid to exhibit entrepreneurial pride. Commitment to the company's values is a responsibility for any top executive. These values, whether innovation, dynamism, the promotion of new activities or job creation, are in fact powerful and deserving of support. French society has suffered from a negative vision of entrepreneurship. As President of the *Mouvement des Entreprises de France* (MEDEF[1]) until 2005, I have led the battle these past years for entrepreneurs to be able to affirm more openly the values which guide them. I know that this is not easy. Companies, indeed, suffer from a relatively negative image in our country. Each challenge or difficulty is hung out to dry. We are quick to mention lay-offs, harassment issues? We content ourselves with a situation of permanent conflict. I believe that other countries have better understood the need for a real partnership between those who

---

1. The leading French employers' association.

govern and those who produce, between the political sphere and companies. This approach is even more crucial given that, as I stated above, our responsibility is collective.

What concrete changes has the emergence of Corporate Responsibility brought about in your company? And what further changes are to come?

Wendel Investissement, like many companies, is operating with more and more transparency. The group has made significant efforts to make itself known to all of its stakeholders, and particularly the public. Our strategy is clear, as are our operations. I was also one of the first to support transparency of salaries. I published my own and I asked the other company executives to do the same, explaining that we had to live up to the level of our remuneration, just as excesses should be condemned.

Concerning our financial commitments, I am very proud of Wendel Investissement' participation in Bureau Veritas, an international leader in certification, quality control and conformity to standards, which strongly contributes to truthfulness in all economic processes. Similarly, from a purely ethical viewpoint, we refused in the past to invest in the tobacco sector when we were involved in the capital of the bioMérieux pharmaceutical laboratory.

Finally, our involvement in research and education has led us to create and finance the "International Wendel Centre for the study of large family firms" at the INSEAD graduate school. Its purpose is the study of the major characteristics of companies whose capital and management remain in the hands of founding families.

How are these changes beneficial to today's companies in terms of finance, management and sales?

In our profession as investors, reputation plays a major role. Trust influences transactions, and through our practice and our culture, Wendel Investissement has succeeded in inspiring this trust. Our partners know that the corporate development strategy in which we invest takes precedence over a purely patrimonial vision. Our image has contributed to the very successful operations which we have carried out these past years: Legrand, Editis, and more recently Materis and Deutsch. Image is now a real economic asset. In fact, nowadays if a company dared declare itself today against the rules of good management, it would be strongly condemned by the media and public opinion. In the current environment, a reputation can be destroyed very quickly.

All of these new rules are, of course, restrictive. But they do not, to my way of thinking, represent a true risk. If stock-market operations become too complex, or too heavy a yoke, then we will simply see stronger development of the unlisted sector. In any case, no yoke can stifle economic freedom.

How would you rate the public image of companies and CEOs in today's society?

The situation in France is somewhat paradoxical. The country wants entrepreneurs, and constantly calls on them to invest and create employment. At the same time, we daily allow ourselves the luxury of denouncing them. This state of affairs is particularly surprising, in that surveys in the field indicate employees are strongly supportive of their companies. It is the media images which are negative, arising from the fact that a certain number of people do not accept the market economy. Because Marxism is not perceived today as a credible alternative, these individuals simply seek to weaken companies through permanent criticism. The difficulty lies in the lack of alternative. Thus, we hear the slogan: "Another world is possible." But no one ever explains what this world would be or how it would be organized. In the meantime, incessant criticism of companies is prejudicial to the economy and to society as a whole.

Werner Wenning
Chairman of the Board of Management of Bayer AG

"Ensure responsible management across the entire
value creation chain."

To whom and how are today's companies accountable?

These days, major companies in the international arena, such as
Bayer, may be integrated into an extremely complex network of
relationships with all interest groups operating in society. In view of
that, it becomes clear that these companies are facing responsibility to
a considerable extent. Summarizing, I would therefore say that
companies today bear responsibility towards all of their many stakeholders.

This attitude corresponds to what I see as constituting the value of a
company. For me, corporate value can certainly not be measured by
the share price alone, as might have been the case in the past. Instead,
I am convinced that to assess the value of a company we have to
consider all the benefits that it brings to its employees and society and
the environment. In other words, we should look not just at the
shareholder value but also at the stakeholder value, which of course
cannot be measured exactly in dollars, yen or euros.

If we take a closer look at the individual stakeholders, we will naturally
realize that a stock market-listed company is primarily accountable to
its stockholders. However, a responsible attitude towards employees is
a top priority too. And, at the end of the day, the scope of Corporate
Responsibility stretches across the entire value-creation chain, from
suppliers and other business partners to customers and consumers.
Being part of society, it lies furthermore within the responsibility of
companies to show a particular interest in society's needs and to be
active in the social sphere as good corporate citizens.

As the top manager of a major corporation, how do you personally experience this responsibility?

I take the issue of responsibility very seriously. It is in my opinion an absolute *sine qua non* for successful collaboration within our company. My own motto is to live what our management demands from our workforce.

What I expect from myself and our employees is that we live our common values every day and that everyone take responsibility for this in their own sphere of activity. The adoption of common values is of prime importance in this context, because they form the basis for a corporate culture that is indeed lived.

Among our central values are therefore "the will to succeed," "respect for people and nature" and "the sustainability of our actions." These and other values are an integral part of our mission statement.

Do you believe today's top executives have to lead by example vis-a-vis their employees and vis-a-vis their community or society as a whole?

Yes. Nothing is as convincing as exemplary behaviour. That is why I believe that top executives must live the values they represent in their daily actions. Or let me put it in other words: walk the talk.

What concrete changes has the emergence of Corporate Responsibility brought about in your company? And what further changes are to come?

I would like first of all to stress that at Bayer, Corporate Responsibility and, more specifically, Corporate Social Responsibility have a tradition going back more than 100 years. As long ago as 1877 the company set up the beginnings of what was to become a company health insurance fund, in 1901 a waste-water commission was established, and in 1905 the first company kindergarten was launched. Our founding fathers thus set a good example.

In the years to follow we continually expanded our social activities in parallel to our economic globalization. We now support some 300 Corporate Social Responsibility projects around the world – quite an impressive number, in my opinion. Within this commitment, we set strategic priorities in the areas of education and research, environmental protection, basic social needs, culture and sports.

Over the course of time, society's expectations of companies have steadily risen and relations with individual interest groups have become ever more complex. We have taken account of this development ment internally by constantly optimizing our organizational structures. For example, we have set up a Sustainability Board under the leadership of the member of the management board responsible for Innovation, Technology and Environment. This committee decides on our objectives, strategies and initiatives in the areas of Sustainable Development and Corporate Social Responsibility, and is supported on an operational basis by a dedicated working group.

As I mentioned at the beginning, the matter of ensuring responsible management along the entire value creation chain is more important than ever for the companies of today. In this context, supplier management plays an important role, and I also consider it a good example of how Corporate Responsibility has changed and daily influences our business. Some time ago we drew up a catalogue of criteria at Bayer which obliges our suppliers to comply with social, ethical and ecological standards. This issue will in my opinion continue to gain in significance in future, especially for globally operating companies.

When considering Corporate Responsibility, one must not, of course, forget the areas of Corporate Compliance and Corporate Governance. The rules and practice of good management and legal compliance among all employees are essential prerequisites of successful operations. That's why, for example, I welcomed the adoption of the German Corporate Governance Code, the enactment of which can lead to greater transparency and trust on the part of investors, customers, employees and the public. This code too is an example of the increased demands on Corporate Responsibility – compliance with it forms part of our daily work processes. The same applies to our Corporate Compliance program, which we launched at the end of the 20th century and through which we regularly update our guidelines of legal compliance and Corporate Responsibility that apply worldwide across the Group.

How are these changes beneficial to today's companies?

Today, our business partners and consumers pay much more attention to purchasing products manufactured by socially and ecologically responsible companies. In recent years Corporate Social Responsibility has no longer been seen as merely a "social case" and an important element for fostering image, but increasingly as a "business case" as well. My view that in the long term social commitment contributes to the success and value of a company has therefore been confirmed.

The financial market has also stepped onto the bandwagon. Share indices have been launched that base their listings on the sustainability performance of companies. Bayer stock is continuously included in important CSR indices such as the Dow Jones Sustainability Indices and the FTSE4Good. For its reduction of emitted greenhouse gases by more than 70 percent since the beginning of the 1990s, Bayer has also been rated "Best in Class" in the Climate Leadership Index – the world's first climate-protection stock index, set up four years ago.

And last but not least, our employees identify particularly with a company and its management that not only treats them fairly but also seeks to meet the demands of society.

How would you rate the public image of companies and CEOs in today's society?

That is a somewhat delicate question, especially when it is directed to a CEO. Top executives are mainly seen as efficient and creative, but sometimes they are also considered to be too distant from the shop floor. In my day-to-day work I try to correspond to the former and disprove the latter.

How companies are perceived generally seems to be ambiguous, as well: on the one hand they provide for material prosperity and offer jobs and personal development opportunities. But on the other, some people consider them to be too much oriented to making profits rather than concerning themselves with the interests of people. I take these views seriously. For me it is essential that people understand that economic success is the basis on which companies can work to the benefit of their employees and society. Such behaviour is honoured accordingly by the public.

Yang Yuanqing
Chairman of the Board of Lenovo

"Integrity is the cornerstone."

To whom and how are today's companies accountable?

Lenovo is at once a new company and an old one. The original Lenovo was created in a small bungalow in Beijing in 1984 to commercialize IT research results in China. In fact, we introduced the PC to households in China. Ten years after our founding, we listed on the Hong Kong Stock Exchange and within a few years, we became China's leading PC supplier. From the very beginning, Lenovo was a unique, pioneering company, focused on satisfying customers and achieving sustained growth and profitability with a market-driven approach.

The new Lenovo was born in 2005, when we acquired the PC Division of IBM. While we had previously been primarily a Chinese company, we have now become a truly global player. Our corporate headquarters is in the United States, our factories and research-and-development facilities ("Innovation Centres") are spread across China, Japan and the US, and our people are located worldwide.

As we build this new Lenovo and forge a new culture from our strong dual heritage, we are accountable to numerous stakeholders on a global scale.

Our top priority is our customers. We pledge to help them be more productive professionally and to enhance their personal lives. Honouring this pledge is essential to our success as a company. As one of the world's largest PC brands, we serve a large and varied customer base which includes large, multinational corporations, small and medium-sized businesses and, in China, a large consumer market.

Because much of our sales comes through indirect channels, we are accountable to the distributors, wholesalers and resellers who are our business partners; our success is inextricably linked to theirs.

We are accountable to our people: the more than 21,000 people worldwide who make up the Lenovo Group. To them, we are committed to provide not only a healthy, safe and pleasant workplace, but also opportunities for both professional and personal growth. Furthermore, because our employees own more than 30 percent of Lenovo shares, we are doubly accountable to them.

Likewise, we are accountable to our external shareholders – including private investors, who own one-third of Lenovo stock – as well as the large US-based institutional investors and other public investors who hold nearly one-quarter of our shares. In addition to providing a satisfactory return on our shareholders' investments, it is our duty to keep the shareholders fully informed of our performance, as well as of our projects and results.

Finally, with research & development labs, plants, logistics centres and offices in 66 countries, we are committed to fulfilling our role as a responsible, active corporate citizen by contributing, both directly and indirectly, to the development of society in every location where we do business.

As the top-manager of a major corporation, how do you personally live this responsibility?

The combination of the leading Asian computer products company focused in China and the strong international customer base and resources of the former IBM PC Division has had dramatic impact upon the Lenovo organization. Both IBM and Lenovo China have a long history of innovative thinking. When you combine this history with our unique, unprecedented situation, it becomes clear that our future depends on our individual and collective ability to find new ideas and innovative solutions. That helps explain why our motto, both internally and externally, is "New World. New Thinking."

In terms of corporate responsibility, we must find innovative approaches as we grow into our new role as a leading global player. Practically, we are identifying the best people, practices, resources and ideas in the company, regardless of origin or location, and building upon these strengths. In the arena of corporate social responsibility, as in all of the other key corporate functions, my job is to make sure that the best people serve on the management team and that they get the support and authority they need to take risks and act decisively, consistent with our objective to be a leader among global corporations. To achieve this, we have instituted a corporate-wide performance-measurement system, encompassing everyone in the organization, at all levels. This formal, uniform, ongoing process ensures that every employee always finds himself or herself on the same, level playing field.

As a global company, Lenovo is very diverse internationally. In addition to Chinese and Americans, the senior leadership team includes people from the Indian subcontinent and Europe. Because we are convinced that diversity is a strength, we continue to bring in senior managers who are neither from IBM nor the "old" Lenovo.

In contrast to some multinational companies, we have appointed women to serve as our CFO and COO of our Product Group. From top to bottom, we are building an organization that is diverse in origin, experience, skills and styles. I believe this is one way we will come up with the innovative, "out of the box" thinking that is vital to our success.

Do you believe today's top-executives have to lead by example vis-a-vis their employees and vis-a-vis their community or society as a whole?

I couldn't agree more. When I joined Lenovo in 1988, right after graduate school, my first job was as a salesperson for workstations. My first customer was a Chinese government representative who needed a PC for some rather simple financial management. Instead, I sold them a high-performance workstation. The sale was a great success for me, but I still regret it. I did learn two important lessons, however: you must understand the customer's needs and sell with integrity.

Today, as all of our senior executives promote leadership values within Lenovo, integrity is one of the three cornerstones that continue to guide us. This is especially important within the Chinese context: when China began the transition from a planned to a market economy, corruption and unethical conduct were widespread in both private companies and state-owned enterprises.

The second cornerstone is the willingness and desire to learn. Personally, I learn from books, from our business partners and suppliers, and from consultants and competitors. I tell Lenovo managers to reserve at least an hour per day for reading. But most importantly, I tell them to learn from their mistakes.

Third, success depends on perseverance, as demonstrated by Lenovo's own success. Who would have thought that a company started by a handful of computer scientists in a Beijing bungalow in 1984 would be the world's third largest PC Company just ten years later?

I often describe the leadership model using a tree analogy: integrity is the root, the base for everything. Perseverance to win constitutes the trunk. The desire to learn is like the leaves, which help absorb nutrients. It takes all three to grow, or to lead.

What are the main tangible changes that the emergence of Corporate Social Responsibility has brought up in the working of your company? And what do you believe are the main changes to come?

In our case, the emergence of Corporate Social Responsibility coincides with our own emergence as a leading global player. Our policies and practices continue to evolve as we assume our new role. This does not mean we shirked our responsibilities previously, however. For example, in 2003, at the height of the SARS epidemic in China, Lenovo donated funds to support SARS prevention, with employees voluntarily raising additional donations for this important cause. In 2005, we contributed to South Asian countries devastated by the tsunami.

More recently, as part of our ongoing corporate citizenship program, we pledged to donate $1 million in computer equipment to Opportunity International, which provides microfinancing for programs in Africa, Asia, Latin America and Eastern Europe. Furthermore, as part of our involvement in the 20th Olympic Winter Games in Italy in 2006, we provided technology and technicians for the Paralympics Winter Games; equipped special lounges to help keep athletes, coaches and staff connected to family and friends during the Paralympics Games; and coordinated a charity event with an organization that helps children in developing countries.

We have always been a pioneer in China, implementing numerous groundbreaking benefits programs, such as our Housing Loan Plan, Vacation Abroad Plan, Employee Stock Ownership Plan and Complementary Medical Insurance. Recently, we became the first company to register our corporate pension program with the Department of Labour and Social Security, as part of an enhanced retirement-benefits initiative.

Finally, I'd like to underscore our particular responsibilities as an IT company. For our customers, we believe it is our responsibility to ensure maximum security and protection for their information and privacy, and we have developed industry-leading technologies to achieve this. In addition, we provide financial support and serve as a technical advisor and board member for StopBadware.org, an initiative launched by Harvard University's Berkman Centre and the Oxford Internet Institute to combat spyware and adware.

We are also committed to the protection of intellectual property, because innovation lies at the very heart of our long-term strategy. All Lenovo employees must get formal permission to use non-Lenovo proprietary materials such as copyrights, patents or trademarks. Furthermore, we recently launched a new initiative in partnership with Microsoft to ensure the universal use of legal software.

How are these changes beneficial to today's companies?

Our entire approach is designed to achieve sustainable, long-term growth and profitability. All of our programs and initiatives in the corporate social responsibility domain support this sustainable-development goal.

In human resources, for example, we have implemented a range of policies and programs to ensure that our people enjoy a safe and healthy workplace. Corporate policies also ensure protection of privacy, workforce diversity and non-discrimination, and controls against conflicts of interest.

Our corporate policy on environmental affairs is designed to provide long-term benefits to people inside and outside the company. Our global environmental-management system helps us achieve results consistent with environmental leadership and ensures that we remain vigilant in protecting the environment across all of our operations worldwide.

How would you rate the public image of companies and CEOs in today's society?

The image of the senior manager is closely related to the image of the company. Indeed, it is one of the key components of the overall corporate image. Of course, corporate images vary widely. However, we can identify a few qualities that generally characterize successful companies: strong social responsibility, a clear development strategy, a focus on the long-term development and a great commitment to public service. All of these can be represented through the senior manager's actions, which provide a visible vehicle for the company's activities and practices.

In the long run, any company's image depends on the underlying reality of the organization and, specifically, the particular set of values shared by the people of the company. When the two organizations that constitute Lenovo were brought together, we asked people to identify the values most critical to their current and future goals. We were surprised by the commonality of the results. People everywhere

emphasized customer focus, strong leadership, clear strategy and effi-
ciency. We built upon this broadly shared heritage to define the values
that would constitute the roots for our new joint culture: the serving of
customers, accuracy and truth-seeking, trustworthiness and integrity,
innovation and entrepreneurship.

Lenovo really is different from other companies. I am convinced that
we are blazing new trails and, ideally, establishing new models for the
future. The values just mentioned provide the foundation for our
company image, internally and externally. As our still-young culture
develops, it will be up to each and every Lenovo employee to bring
these values to life on a daily basis. As they do so, people everywhere
will instinctively identify Lenovo with these values.

When I meet with Lenovo people around the world, I never try to
paint over the real differences that exist among us. Rather, I tell my
people that we need to understand these differences and use them to
our advantage, allowing us to reach acceptable compromises.

As we integrate our cultures, one of our most valuable resources is our
ability to listen. This same skill will enable us to respond satisfactorily
to all of the various stakeholders to whom we are accountable.

Nicole Notat
President of Vigeo

"Accountability is a management choice."

To whom and how are today's companies accountable?

The issue of corporate responsibility dates back to the beginnings of companies themselves. It seems to me to imply two major lines of questioning: what is the purpose of the company? For whom does it act?

Two opposing conceptualizations exist. The first places companies at the service of society, benefactors of sorts for all of their stakeholders.

At the other end of the spectrum is a vision which I would qualify as "Friedmanesque," in which companies are seen as accountable only to their shareholders. Any use of dividends which does not contribute to enriching shareholders, rather than other stakeholders, would be seen as contrary to the interests of the company.

Clearly, this conception is not the one which my agency seeks to promote. We aim to present a partnership vision of the company which, certainly, acknowledges shareholders' essential role, but which also highlights the importance of other stakeholders.

From this perspective, the idea of "social" responsibility is limiting. Talking about "societal" responsibility is more accurate. A responsible company is one which takes into account the interests of all stakeholders from a managerial viewpoint. I want to be clear on this point: this is not a moralizing vision. It is a management choice on the part of executives. It is up to management to define how far to go in considering stakeholders' interests, and to what extent the company is accountable to them.

Companies are not required to consider the demands of every interest group. I repeat: it is a choice, a management decision.

Within the framework of this "collective" corporate responsibility, how do you perceive top executives' personal accountability? Do you believe they have an obligation to their employees? To society as a whole?

We expect executives to be able to translate their vision of the company and its development into policies and practices which demonstrate a real commitment to stakeholders' interests. They must, in this area, go beyond declarations and ensure that this societal responsibility structures the organization and its management.

I believe that the implementation of these principles is a necessity for companies. I am not speaking here of moral obligations or the desire to set an example. I am convinced (and many recent studies also show) that fulfilling shareholders' long-term interests requires companies to take concrete notice of the interests of other stakeholders, whether employees, clients, suppliers, or the natural or regional environment.

This idea is nothing new. It guided the work of the large entrepreneurs of the past. We could mention, for example, Antoine Riboud, for whom economic and financial performance indicators had to be considered in tandem with equally strong social and societal criteria. Or Jean Gandois on the topic of the citizen-company.

Some executives, in contrast, considered for a long time that "externalities" resulting from decisions of the company were in no way their responsibility. I believe that this is changing today. There is a growing consensus around the idea that companies are responsible for the consequences of their activities on their environment. We could use the example of the shutting down of an industrial site: today it is considered "normal" for the company closing the site to contribute to the training and possibly the rehabilitation and relocation of the workers whose jobs are lost. This goes beyond the individual responsibility of the top executive. It must be seen as a collective responsibility on the part of management as a whole, for any consequence of decisions made by the company.

Companies which badly manage these external consequences expose themselves to risk, in terms not only of image, but also of the cohesiveness of their human capital. These companies also become markedly less attractive to clients and future collaborators. One of the paradoxes of the much-maligned globalization, in my opinion, is that it allows for an upward levelling of social and societal practices by "suppliers," under pressure from their large multinational clients, which are themselves carefully monitored by better informed, more mature and demanding consumers and public opinion.

A word on the role-model ideal, which is often attributed to top executives. A top manager may be motivated by greed to an excessive degree, but large companies have boards of directors and wages committees with a job to do. Here again, we are witness to a collective responsibility, within which each individual must apply his or her own values of accountability.

In your opinion, what concrete changes has the emergence of Corporate Responsibility brought about in companies? And what further changes are to come?

Numerous tangible and concrete signs show how the theme has penetrated the corporate world today.

The first visible indicator is the creation of sustainable development, and professional ethics committees. The second is the evolution of information provided in annual reports or sustainable-development reports. Through a ripple effect, access to this information has led companies to make significant investments in creating adequate reporting systems.

I would add to this list the efforts made by a growing number of companies in identifying all their stakeholders, and in bringing them together and keeping them informed.

Finally, in my profession, I observe that more and more companies are turning to us for Corporate Responsibility audits. This suggests, I believe, a growing consciousness on the part of management that they must evaluate their performance in this area, too, and that the conclusions of our audits can be strategic governing tools for them.

How are these changes beneficial to today's companies?

First, there are still companies for which accountability issues and practices are primarily a source of additional costs. This is an idea which must be corrected.

Primarily because, very directly, there are areas in which sustainable-development issues offer considerable development opportunities.

I am thinking in particular of waste management, recycling and treatment, and the eco-conception of products. I am also thinking of the automobile industry, with the arrival of "clean" or renewable energy.

These areas represent very significant sources of added value and wealth creation. There are costs, certainly, but these are research-and-development investments which will generate growth.

Second, while we may not be able to measure the benefit of "responsible" behaviour in financial terms, we will one day be able to measure the cost of negligence. It seems to me that there is a parallel to be drawn with the attitude which many companies had towards employee training twenty years ago, when it was viewed as a cost, an investment with no return.

Today, in view of increased competition, professional mobility and technological and demographic change, these same companies understand that employee training is a crucial issue.

I believe that a similar transformation will occur as regards social, or societal, responsibility. This theme will very soon be seen as an opportunity by a majority of companies. Because a responsible company's products and services will be more attractive to citizen-consumers, because the company's attitude and practices vis-à-vis its environment will be selection criteria for possible future employees... and because investors also watch companies' mastery of these new social and environmental risks.

It seems to me, therefore, that in the globalised context in which we operate today, a company, particularly an international one, will be unable to ignore these expectations.

How would you rate the public image of companies and CEOs in today's society?

Here in France we are facing a paradox. When we ask employees about their degree of satisfaction with their own companies, the results are excellent. When we question them about companies in general, however, they express very negative opinions.

How can we explain this gap? I believe that corporate executives have neglected to explain and communicate concerning the role of their companies, their accomplishments and the use of their profits. We in France live with a persistently unflattering vision of the entrepreneurial sphere, which is viewed as cynical, predatory and interested only in short-term profit. In view of certain recent events, we are forced to admit that this negative image is not always without justification.

Still, companies on the whole do not merit this bad reputation. I come back to what I mentioned above: corporate executives must make significant efforts towards gaining the public's trust; the public opinion battle is the one they must win.

What leads today's companies to request a Corporate Responsibility evaluation from a rating agency such as Vigeo?

When I launched this project three years ago, I thought that the communication pressures on companies would be their primary motivation. This has proved to be wrong.

What companies want above all is external feedback: are they in line – and how effectively? – with what is expected of them in this area? Through our audits, they receive the most objective response possible. I am also satisfied to note that our conclusions are often followed by the implementation of action plans designed to reduce the exposed inefficiencies.

I also note that a social audit is a strong mobilizing force within the company. Concrete commitment to a strategic project which reconciles economic performance and consideration of social and societal interests is a uniting factor for human resources, one which is not implemented only in response to a crisis.

Demand is on the rise today. A new dynamic is forming. Certainly, we work essentially with large companies, and much remains to be done, but I am convinced that medium-sized companies in sectors in which sustainable-development issues exist are already aware of the benefits this can bring.

CONCLUSIONS

How do we educate for responsibility?

1) Multiple meanings of "responsibility"

The authors of these different contributions, experienced managers of large companies, answered the same questions. The variation in their replies highlights the multiple meanings of the word "responsibility", as it is used today to describe responsibility for and responsibilities of a company. Before examining how to teach responsibility, we should therefore explore the multiple meanings and uses of this word.

In the variations on answers to the first question, a semantic question arises which is more difficult in the French language than in English. "*Responsabilité*" (adjective: "*responsable*") in French is used to translate indiscriminately the English words "responsibility" and "accountability" (adjectives: "responsible" and "accountable"). The concept of "accountability" is precise: it means "to give an accounting"; that is, to answer for one's actions, particularly from a perspective of loyalty and transparency. It is a moral duty to say what we do. "*Responsabilité*" in French also carries this meaning of a debt owed, in addition to the other meanings of the word, as richly layered in English as in French: in both languages, it can just as easily refer to the legal meaning, which answers the question "Who is responsible?" (to carry personal responsibility for a part of the company's actions *vis-à-vis* external parties) as the sense of a moral order, of a responsible attitude or behavior, of taking responsibility, and of a responsible commitment towards others.

Etymologically, "responsible" means "to respond" (answer) for something to someone, the one answering for his or her actions doing so legally as well as morally or practically ("to give an accounting"). Let us now consider the diversity of answers to the questions "To whom, and how, are today's companies accountable?"

To the question "To whom?", the most frequently cited items are, in decreasing order, responsibility towards shareholders, employees, clients, those affected directly or indirectly by the company's activities and suppliers (mentioned by only one of the authors). Given the ever-increasing attention paid to the notion of an integrated value-creation chain, the neglect of suppliers is an interesting point: how can suppliers be treated fairly, and using what criteria, when half of a company's profits today might result from buyers putting suppliers in competition with one another...? The responsibility training which we are discussing will depend on how the perimeter of a company's responsibilities is defined.

Defining this perimeter leads us to examine the company's *raison d'être*, and here again we can see important variations in interpretation, as Nicole Notat points out: among the authors, some content themselves with creating value for shareholders, if possible without negative environmental, social or economic impact in the short or medium term. For others, it is *"society as a whole which invests companies with the mission of satisfying a certain number of fundamental individual and collective needs, in particular the creation of wealth and jobs"* (E.-A. Seillière). To approach the issue of training, at this stage we will retain the definition of a company's purpose, formulated by the UN and EFMD (European Foundation for Management Development) working group on Globally Responsible Leadership: *"The role of a globally responsible company is to create economic and societal progress in a sustainable and globally responsible way"*.

2) Educating for responsibility

Our experience at ESSEC Business School shows us that a broad audience, from 20 to 45 years old, wishes to explore these ideas: the world is too complex, and change takes place too rapidly for the highest performers to take the time to understand this environment.

Educate whom, and at what age?

This question is anything but trivial. Different visions compete in the international arena regarding how and when to teach responsibility in business. The United States and Britain offer full-time MBA programs after two to eight years of professional experience. Students returning to campus are rich in experience, but not always in understanding, and show a strong appetite for discovering new concepts. It is seeing their concrete experiences in light of their new understanding that leads to personal reflection. While not without value, this approach to education has the drawback of taking place at a time when young adults' values are already fairly anchored, and when a certain number of them want this education only for its instrumental and operational content, without intending to profoundly examine their own attitudes, values or behaviors.

In other models, an earlier business education is preferred, which allows us to accompany students into young adulthood at the very moment that they are making their first personal decisions, to expose them to experiences they might not otherwise have chosen, to alternate these experiences with the concepts with which to process them. Among other things, we can work with a more balanced public in terms of sex (between 22 and 25 years of age, women make up 50% of a class; between 28 and 30 years, they are only 15 to 20%), offer more choice and longer experiences, and above all develop an integrated sense of complex questions, as the students are prepared earlier to examine a situation in all its complexity.

We believe, however, that the most interesting, even the most challenging public is the younger students, as they must pass through every phase of an education for responsibility: the methods developed here must be very complete, given this group's inexperience, and if they prove efficient can often be adapted to a more experienced public.

Making responsibility desirable through the success of those responsible

To instill a culture of responsibility in college-age students, one necessary step is to cultivate the desire to take or accept responsibility. Student life provides much opportunity for this. What students currently carrying responsibilities will say of the balance between pleasure and pain in exercising these will be decisive for their successors. It is thus essential to this goal that university instructors, in their permanent and sometimes conflictual dialogue with responsible students, always keep in mind that their role is to accompany these young people with the aim of making student responsibility interesting, motivating and a source of success for the students. In this way, students will be attracted to responsibility, real pressure for job selection will take place and the circle will be virtuous. It is scarcely necessary to point out the disastrous effects of a position of power which is too unappealing to attract high-quality people, and the importance of ensuring, in contrast, that all due attention is paid to fostering this attractiveness. The key is to motivate students through their predecessors' success.

The corollary is, of course, to accompany those who at any given moment hold responsibilities. Students can discover the joys of legal and penal responsibility, of regulating the behavior of large groups, of accident management, and they experience the normal doubts of new leaders. The way in which *we* support them, without occupying their place, provides them with very specific lessons on important issues.

Within these phases, exercising responsibility sometimes makes it clear that ambition is the only motivation, a "vain" one; that is, only for its own sake. These positive crises (etymologically, "*Krisis*", in Greek = passage), if they are treated with tact and openness, will be effective pedagogical tools.

Finally, whatever the tendency to take responsibility or not within the student milieu, it is essential that all be expected to take full responsibility for their own studies. Offering a large range of very different choices, and the consequences required by these choices, is a powerful tool for training students in *choosing*; that is, deciding: this is a foundation of responsible behavior.

Educating for "global" responsibility: changing perspectives through experiencing complexity

Whether or not students take on specific responsibilities, understanding broader responsibility comes largely through discovering the real world's tensions and aggression, the contradictory and yet legitimate aspirations of various stakeholders. Experiencing personal destabilization, whether in a foreign country or an unfamiliar and confusing social milieu, or both, is what creates lucid and enlightened world citizens: such experiences lead them to understand other viewpoints or perspectives of a single situation, and may lead to a completely different understanding; this means seeing the world through others' eyes.

Not all students are ready for the same experiences, and professors must show discernment. But the power of experiential teaching is without equal. The daughter of a Parisian lawyer who spends three months herding sheep on horseback in New Zealand with local shepherds returns transformed, as does the son of an urban pharmacist who spends two months helping to build a dispensary in rural India. Discovering the realities of the *banlieues* (lower-income suburbs) is no less destabilizing. The work of certain humanitarian associations (ATD Quart Monde, in particular) with young engineering students, the ESSEC prison visitors' program and others have very long-term impacts.

This type of trajectory can help students discover the consequences of companies' decisions along the entire value-creation chain and on the economic and social environment influenced by these decisions; the pedagogical effect is maximized. The approach leads, above all, to understanding the extraordinary variety of mental representations of a same issue.

It is desirable for such experiences to illustrate the strength of social inequality, and its consequence for the planet's environmental situation: students will develop the desire to understand the macroscopic facets to these issues, yet always with the risk of not progressing beyond the phase of emotional perception. Thus, making responsibility desirable, educating for an understanding of the complexity of situations which contribute to an enlightened and responsible attitude, are essential teaching objectives.

3) Educating for an ethical sense

Recognizing ethical dilemmas

Students, like managers, may refuse to accept responsibility through fear of having to deal with difficult choices, situations in which too many opposing interests are at play. This fear is healthy when it leads to a lucid understanding; it is detrimental when it paralyzes decision-making.

Our experience shows that we can move students beyond fear simply by giving them practice in taking decisions in ethically conflicting situations. With practice, they will be less fearful of finding themselves in such situations, as they will consider these normal; they will have identified certain personal keys which will help them settle ethical dilemmas and recognize the contingent nature of their decisions, often made on a 55/45 basis; decision which it is not worth "hanging themselves" for even if it turns out to be mistaken.

Training to manage these dilemmas

Through the interplay of personal or collective roles, through case studies, the student is obligated to make choices, and then to account for these to his or her peers. Students or participants (in the case of professional training) thus discover their implicit values, their spontaneous reflexes, towards issues which they would prefer never to have addressed. These lessons are powerful for uncovering their instinctive reactions, which will often be perceived as reassuring and coherent with regard to a sense of self, if sometimes as dissonant and requiring intense self-examination (e.g., "I didn't think I would be capable of reacting that way; this doesn't suit me at all, so how can I change if this is my spontaneous reaction?"). In general, these lessons lead to a certain introspective approach to better understand the students' reactions and to refine their internal compass.

In debates which occur during these lessons, participants also have the opportunity to discover three essential elements:

- The strength and legitimacy of arenas of collective debate for regulating the social group: the practical application of Jürgen Habermas's theory of communication acts.
- The powerful conditioning of personal choices and opinions by people's social roles at any given time: observing that "I think as I act" is closer to reality than "I act as I think", which is often an upsetting discovery;
- The strength of internal or external codes for modeling behavior, and thus the levers for corporate culture which these codes can be.

Between educating for responsibility and teaching a sense of ethics, the professions are evolving.

The complexity of economic and social relations also engenders a rapid development of professions whose very function is to regulate the system, independent third parties guaranteeing transactional equity: certified accountants, auditors, tribunal experts, market-regulation authorities, rating agencies, business attorneys, all of these professions are expanding rapidly. The real historical mark of the Enron affair was not Enron itself, but the death of Arthur Andersen in a few short months.

The professions have very specific shared characteristics. For example, they are called "independent", meaning that an external independent perspective, critical and often public, is integral to the service provided to the client (and for which the client pays).

They are also generally structured by professional codes of ethics, "a set of rules and requirements which regulate a profession, the conduct of those who exercise it, and the relationship between these former and their clients or the public" (Petit Larousse). These are often professions organized around an "Order" (doctors, lawyers, certified accountants, architects) in which the order or association's principal mission is to preserve the founding principles of the profession, often even delivering a "right to exercise" which measures both competence and moral integrity, thus acting as a veritable guardian of ethical conduct.

We mention these professions here, at the crossroads of teaching responsibility and teaching a sense of ethics, because companies in these sectors are often considered to be interesting places to begin a career; they serve as "incubators" for future leaders, and their educational dimension should not be underestimated.

The quality of behavioral training, the fundamental concepts which leaders in these professions transmit, will thus have an influence which is much larger than in the professionals' own fields. It is therefore not surprising that Mazars, for its anniversary, chose to reflect on these questions.

Recognizing ethical dilemmas, training people to deal with them, giving particular consideration to independent professions structured around professional codes of conduct and which train a number of future leaders are, to our mind, the main areas to explore in teaching a sense of ethics.

4) The support of major modern authors

The lessons which we have mentioned are above all behavioral. This is why real-life situations, whether in role-playing or in longer experiences, are the premier teaching tools.

Brilliant students or top executives are not satisfied with this situational training, although they do find great value in it: they also seek a deeper understanding and intellectual coherence through the study of certain major modern authors, who built their philosophical reflection on questions of ethics and responsibility. This type of knowledge nourishes students and participants by allowing them to gain additional distance; in theorizing about the elements of the decision-making process, they extend the lesson more largely to future unknown situations.

Hans Jonas, Emmanuel Lévinas, Jürgen Habermas and John Rawls are some of the most important writers in this field. They complement one another remarkably and leave each of us the freedom to find our own path between their conceptualizations. Let us attempt to briefly summarize the essential points.

Hans Jonas: Imperative of Responsibility

Jonas founded the concepts of sustainable development, respectful of a natural environment threatened by technology.

For Jonas, who contrasts an ethics of conviction (my actions are the consequence of my convictions) and an ethics of responsibility (I act according to what seems most responsible at a given time), the Responsibility Imperative is characteristic of a technological society in which rapid development is disquieting; it gives birth to the notion of sustainable development (of natural and human resources); the responsibility principle creates a specific responsibility towards anything vulnerable or threatened. Responsibility is, in fact, the internal debate between our fears and our hopes, with a permanent awareness of our own fragility. It is a personal attitude which leads to action.

Emmanuel Lévinas: Wholeness and Infinity revealed by the face of the other

Lévinas constructs the relationship to the other, personalized, as the source and inspiration of our ethical sense and our responsibility.

Lévinas's main concepts are based on human beings' ability to accept the idea of infinity, of otherness; the encounter between infinity and subjectivity is expressed in the revelation of the face of the other, which exteriorizes this infinity. The face of the other, in its majesty and fragility, constitutes infinity's presence in the ephemeral moment. Attention to the other, whose face invokes my ability to encounter infinity, awakens an awareness of justice, ethical thinking, defense of the good and of the other: to be fully human is to accomplish our existence for others, to be able to see the offence to the offended, the face of the other.

Jürgen Habermas: The communication act

For Habermas, responsibility and the construction of ethics are above all procedural, arising from the communication act between people and groups.

It is necessary, in communicating, to try to construct reasoning which expresses mutual comprehension (inter-comprehension) for members of a given community. The ends and values are not confined previous to communicating; participants seek agreement on a situation, a problem, in order to consensually coordinate their plans and actions. All questions involving differences of perception and understanding must be debated; it is necessary to simultaneously discuss human structures (the system) and realities of the experienced world, as the participants perceive and conceptualize them.

John Rawls: Justice as equity

For Rawls, it is the progress of justice as equity which determines the progress of an ethical consciousness and the field of action for responsible decisions.

Each person, in society or in an organization, must have equal rights to the most extensive system of fundamental freedoms, equal for all; each person's system of fundamental freedoms must be compatible with the same system for the others.

Social and economic inequalities (observed but not considered definitive) must be "organized" (referring to the hierarchy of positions, salaries etc.) in a way which provides the most disadvantaged, the least endowed, with opportunities for the best income and possibilities for advancement: this is the project of society; social and economic inequalities must be attached to functions and positions open to all, in conformity with the principles of equal opportunity (a reference to the fight against discrimination). It is necessary to construct basic principles for social cooperation which benefit everyone, and not just the largest number; this cooperation, based on the recognition of all participants, is seen according to an essentially procedural conceptualization of justice (based on rational and reasonable decisions) which seeks to reduce all conflicts of values.

We see how these four authors examine the question of responsibility from complementary perspectives: Jonas establishes the principle of sustainable development through the duty to protect that which is fragile, Lévinas defines responsibility in relation to other persons, Rawls does so in relation to the desirable aims of a just society, and finally Habermas defines the arena of responsibility by the forms and procedures of collective work.

The pertinence of these four authors in relation to the collected testimonials

It is interesting to observe that, for all the questions asked of these corporate executives, their responses easily connect to each of the above-cited categories.

If we illustrate, for example, with the fourth question asked of these executives, *"What concrete changes has the emergence of Corporate Responsibility brought about in your company?"*, the answers can be described as follows:

For ČEZ, the donor's generosity towards social projects, the consideration of stakeholders in company decisions and the search for renewable energy sources characterize the responsible operation of the company: all four authors are present here.

For HSBC, the concern is to integrate responsibility into all decision-making processes (procedural, Habermas), to commit to carbon neutrality (Jonas), and to include social risk in risk management (Rawls).

AXA is concerned with bringing a sustainable development strategy into the company's actions, including personnel and environment (Jonas), with a commitment to society on these issues (Jonas and Rawls), ideally becoming society's preferred company and thus that of potential clients (Habermas).

For Telefónica, the most pertinent form of Corporate Social Responsibility depends on the country (Rawls, Lévinas); it consists above all of a model for internal change directed towards excellence (Habermas).

For Solvay, CSR should be defined depending on location and time (contingency, Rawls); the environment (Jonas) and social inequality (Rawls, Lévinas) are the challenges of the next twenty years, an internal code of ethics has been written and is regularly reviewed, in particular to define the Solvay culture in new countries of operations (Habermas).

Vodafone aims to create products and services which produce both social and business profits. Creating a team specifically for the diffusion of social responsibility has transformed procedures (Habermas) and highlighted progress margins; the public nature of the audits creates trust, and therefore value (Habermas).

For Wendel Investissement, these changes have led to increased transparency (Habermas), and investment decisions now include consideration of their ethical and social dimension (Rawls).

For Benetton, corporate responsibility must primarily focus on the long term (Jonas); the long-term perspective reconciles interests which, in the short term, may appear contradictory.

On one specific question, with a great diversity of answers, we see how the principles underlying these opinions can easily be referenced to the above-mentioned authors; we could carry out this exercise with every question. The four philosophers make up an extremely solid base for thinking about a responsible attitude.

Conclusion
Corporate responsibility: a necessity or a passing phase?

A convergence of social actors, companies, youth

In a world now as open as it is uncertain, in which high volatility, well known in market finance, affects economic, financial, social and political movements with equal speed and unpredictability, three simultaneous phenomena are apparent:

- Those endowed with social rights demand from companies more and more responsible, transparent, understandable behavior and commitment to sustainable development; growing regulatory and legal constraints on companies are the result.
- Companies know that the best among them are distinguished by their ability to integrate these issues into their service offering, whether through ways of doing things or even the invention of new products or services.
- As educators, we can testify that the most brilliant of our students have the desire to carry out their future profession with these questions in mind.
- They look for companies which address the questions seriously and which take seriously those who wish to include personal, collective and sustainable responsibility in their development trajectory. These young people are both "willing" and "able to take on" responsibilities. They will forge the future around such issues, because these very issues are their own.

Globally responsible leadership

Game theory also helps illuminate this debate, by teaching us that often, if the game is of short duration, it is in players' interest to cheat, while for the longer term, it is in their interest to cooperate and respect the rules of the game. Beyond personal ethical considerations, sustainable development and responsible corporate behavior can now be viewed as rational economic choices.

For all these reasons, considering corporate social responsibility or, in a broader formulation, "globally responsible leadership" as both an obligation for successful companies, and a real economic and organizational opportunity.

Jim Collins, in his popular book *Good to Great*, points out how often exceptionally and continuously successful companies are founded before all else on values. By giving more meaning to their work, globally responsible companies will attract the most brilliant associates.

What remains is to educate future leaders who wish to take on the depth of meaning which we have given the word "responsibility". Our experience leads us to say that this is largely possible, because most intelligent people are often honest and therefore believe that such complex issues are unavoidable if they wish to remain honest towards themselves.

All the players in the company must then choose to educate themselves about these issues, by creating space for freedom and debate which will nourish the associates, in concert with the company's mission.
At times, this may be an opportunity to rethink the mission itself, with a more responsible eye.

Pierre Tapie,
President of ESSEC Business School

The following is an interview with Professor Gilbert Lenssen featured in the May 2006 issue of Ethical Corporation written in partnership with EABIS (European Academy for Business in Society).

What trends in business will drive the future in management education?

Two major trends, globalisation and the widespread adoption of information communication technology, have created an operating environment far more complex and challenging for business than ever before.

How businesses are organised, operate and compete have all undergone, and will continue to undergo, profound changes. As globalisation picks up momentum, the firm is faced with new challenges, including operating in multicultural environments and being forced to navigate complex and varied political environments with a weak or non-existent state. There is more uncertainty and volatility.

Simple corporate philanthropy, on the way to massive profits, is no longer acceptable. A firm's impact on the environment – and the broader economic, cultural and political setting – matters and can bring it competitive advantages, or threaten its survival.

The second major trend is the spread of information technology. Firms have become more embedded with their stakeholders. Distributors, suppliers and even customers have all become interconnected through the Internet and corporate intranets. This has led to a redefinition of "the firm" where it is no longer clear boundaries that hold a company together, but its purpose and identity.

All these add up to a very challenging business environment with many new risks. It is the firms that have managers that can successfully navigate his challenging environment, and turn risk into opportunities, that will flourish in such a volatile age.

How have student expectations and demands of business schools changed?

Student expectations of graduate schools have evolved as the broader business environment has moved towards complex, globalised economies. The key driver of this is the spread of information communication technology.

Historically, business schools and professors have had a monopoly on information. It was they who possessed the knowledge and information and their role was to impart that knowledge to students.

With the massive amounts of information now available online, the traditional role of teachers is being challenged by students who want more than just the transmission of information. They are looking for the cross-functional skills to be able to navigate and manage the intrinsic complexities of a globalised economy. And, so, they want management school models that are based on increased student autonomy with them being more responsible for their own learning.

What are the knowledge, skills and competencies that business will require in the future from management education, and why?

Firms are facing unprecedented pressures and having to cope with issues that were previously tangential to their pursuit of profit. In this new environment, businesses need capable managers that can manage these challenges and risks, and have the skills and insight to turn them into opportunities.

This means adopting policies and strategies that take Corporate Responsibility beyond the defensively oriented and isolated "CSR department" to incorporating it across the firm as a strategic competitive advantage.

To meet this demand from businesses, management education will have to evolve from being tactical and instrument-oriented programmes – that preach the deeply institutionalised mantra that the "business of business is business" – to ones that give managers practical and real strategic insights into the cultural, economic and political environments in which they operate.

More specifically, these are the cross-functional skills to manage stakeholder relations and evaluate the short-term trade offs of Corporate Responsibility and bottom line profit. These will enable students to develop a knowledge of broader social and political systems to identify risks as well as opportunities, a knowledge of environmental issues and laws and, crucially, a clear conception of the role and impact of business in society as a social, political and economic actor.

Professor Gilbert Lenssen,
President of the European Academy for Business in Society (EABIS)

BIOGRAPHIES

César ALIERTA

- César Alierta has been the Chairman and CEO of Telefónica since 2000.
- He was previously president of Tabacalera SA and Logista, a subsidiary of the Altadis group. During his professional career, he also founded and presided over Beta Capital and occupied the function of General Manager of the markets division for the Urquijo bank in Madrid. César Alierta is a member of the board of trustees of Plus Ultra, Terra and Iberia. He has also been an administrator and member of the Standing Committee for the Madrid stock exchange.
- César Alierta today remains the administrator of Altadis, of which he is also a member of the executive committee.
- He received an MBA from Columbia University in New York, and a law degree from the University of Saragossa.

Alessandro BENETTON

- At the age of 42, Alessandro Benetton is the founding president of 21 Investimenti Group, a commercial bank created in 1993 and since then transformed into a private equity company operating in Italy and France.
- Alessandro Benetton is a member of the executive committee and is vice-president of the Board of Directors of Benetton Group SpA, a member of the Boards of Directors of Edizione Holding SpA, Autogrill SA and the Fondazione Rosselli, a research institute based in Turin. He is also a member of the advisory board of Robert Bosch International Beteiligungen AG in Zurich and a member of the Confindustria Committee. Finally, from 1988 to 1998, he was president of Benetton Formula 1.
- Alessandro Benetton holds a Bachelor of Science degree, cum laude, from Boston University. After holding a financial-analyst

position at Goldman Sachs, he earned an MBA from the Harvard Business School.

Martin BOUYGUES

- Martin Bouygues was born in 1952, the year his father, Francis Bouygues, founded Bouygues. In 1974, he joined the Group as a foreman, before entering the company's sales division. In 1979, he created Maison Bouygues, specialized in the sale of family homes by catalogue. In 1984, he actively participated in the acquisition of Saur, a water treatment and distribution company, which he headed two years later. A director of Bouygues since 1982, Martin Bouygues succeeded Francis Bouygues on September 5, 1989, as Chairman and CEO of the Group. During the 1990s, under his guidance, Bouygues continued its development in international construction as well as in communications with the launch of Bouygues Telecom. Today, Bouygues is a diversified industrial group whose activities are organized into two categories: construction, with Bouygues Construction, Bouygues Immobilier and Colas; and media/telecommunications, with TF1 and Bouygues Telecom. Present in 80 countries, the Group has more than 115,400 employees and posted sales of €24.1 billion in 2005.

Patrick de CAMBOURG

- A graduate of the Paris Institute of Political Studies (1971), with additional degrees in literature, government and civil law, chartered accountant and auditor, Patrick de Cambourg began his career as an assistant with Mazars in February 1974 at the age of twenty-four. He became a partner in 1978, and Chairman of Mazars in 1983. He has since regularly been reconfirmed in his position at the head of the organisation.
- Patrick de Cambourg is or has been a member of a variety of committees among the organisations of his profession (Order of Chartered Accountants, French Auditors' Institute, French Accounting Standards Council), and participated in the Le Portz Committee on network ethics. In 2004 and 2005, he chaired the "Public Interest Practice" department of the French Auditors' Institute and the international section of the National Accounting Council. He is a Knight of the National Order of Merit and of the Legion of Honour.

Henri de CASTRIES

- Born in 1954, Henri de Castries has been chairman of the management board and CEO of AXA since May 2000.
- After his secondary studies in Paris, HEC in 1976 and a law degree, Henri de Castries entered the ENA. Upon graduating from the ENA, he opted for the Ministry of Finance. From 1980 to 1984, he carried out audits of various French administrations for the French tax inspectorate. In 1984, he joined the Treasury. In 1986, he participated in corporate privatization. He then took on the responsibility for the foreign-exchange and balance of payments market.
- He joined AXA on September 1, 1989, as part of the Group's central finance division. Nominated secretary general in 1991, he was responsible for the legal restructuring and mergers arising from the integration of the Compagnie du Midi companies. In 1993, nominated Senior Executive Vice President of AXA, he took charge of asset management, finance and real estate companies, and then, in 1994, of the operations in North America and Great Britain. In 1996, he was closely involved in the merger with UAP and the integration of the teams of both groups. In 1997, he was named Chairman of the Board of Directors of Equitable, which would become AXA Financial.
- Henri de Castries is administrator of the "Association pour l'Aide aux Jeunes Infirmes" (assistance for disabled youth) and president of AXA Hearts in Action.

Alain ETCHEGOYEN

- Alain Etchegoyen was born in Lille in 1951. A graduate of the Ecole Normale Supérieure in the rue d'Ulm, he holds a masters in thermodynamics and passed the competitive state exam in philosophy in 1973. Most of his philosophical work, which includes numerous publications, concerns the notion of responsibility.
- He was a philosophy professor at Coulommiers high school (lycée) from 1976 to 1981, then since 1981 in the preparatory classes at Louis le Grand in Paris. In addition, he has taught at the Galilée high school (in a "priority education" zone) in Gennevilliers since 1998 and was the first to occupy the Chair for Business Ethics at the Free University of Brussels (1992-1995).
- Alain Etchegoyen has provided consulting services for companies and unions since 1986. He was the administrator of the Usinor Group after the company's privatization and has been a member of

the Bouygues Telecom Scientific Committee since 2001. From 2003 to 2005, he was Commissioner to the Plan (Commissaire au Plan).

- Finally, he was a member of the National Ethics Committee from 1998 to 2001. He was a member of the Scientific Committee of the ECRIN with the National Council for Scientific Research since 1999, and of the Ethics Committee of the CNAB (National Confederation of Assets Administrators) since 2000.

Adi GODREJ

- Adi Godrej is Chairman and CEO of the Godrej Group. He is also chairman of Godrej Industries Ltd., Godrej Consumer Products Ltd. Godrej Foods Ltd., Godrej Sara Lee Ltd., Godrej Properties Ltd., Godrej Beverages and Foods Ltd. and Keyline Brands Ltd., U.K. The Godrej Group is one of India's largest conglomerates.
- Adi Godrej is a Director of numerous firms, including Godrej & Boyce Mfg. Co. Ltd., Godrej Agrovet Ltd., Godrej International Ltd., Godrej Global MidEast FZE, He is the Chairman of the Board of Trustees of the Dadabhai Naoroji Memorial Prize Fund. He has also chaired several professional associations. Mr. Godrej also serves as a member of the National Council of the Confederation of Indian Industry and is a member of the Governing Board of the Indian School of Business. Mr. Godrej is a recipient of several awards and recognitions including the Rajiv Gandhi Award 2002.
- Adi Godrej received his undergraduate and Master's degree in management from the Massachusetts Institute of Technology.

Stephen GREEN

- Stephen Green is Chairman and Executive Director of HSBC Holdings plc. He was born in England on 7 November 1948.
- Has degrees from Oxford University and the Massachusetts Institute of Technology.
- He began his career with the British Government's Ministry of Overseas Development. In 1977 he joined McKinsey & Co Inc, management consultants, with whom he undertook assignments in Europe, North America and the Middle East.
- He joined The Hong Kong and Shanghai Banking Corporation Limited in 1982 with responsibility for corporate planning activities, and, in 1985, was put in charge of the development of the bank's global treasury operations. In 1992 he became Group

Treasurer of HSBC Holdings plc, with responsibility for the HSBC Group's treasury and capital markets businesses globally.

- In March 1998 he was appointed to the Board of HSBC Holdings plc as Executive Director, Investment Banking and Markets responsible for the investment banking, private banking and asset management activities of the Group. He assumed additional responsibility for the Group's corporate banking business in May 2002. He became Group Chief Executive on 1 June 2003 and Group Chairman on 26 May 2006. He is Chairman of HSBC Bank plc and of HSBC Private Banking Holdings (Suisse) SA.
- He is a director of The Hong Kong and Shanghai Banking Corporation Limited, of HSBC North America Holdings Inc., and of HSBC France.
- Stephen Green is married with two daughters.

Daniel JANSSEN

- Baron Daniel Janssen was born in Brussels in 1936. He received a Civil Engineering degree from the Université Libre de Bruxelles in 1958, and a certificate in Nuclear Physics in 1959. He then obtained an MBA from the Harvard Business School in 1962. He was a Cabinet Attaché at the Euratom Commission in 1959-1960 and an instructor at the Université Libre de Bruxelles from 1965 to 1972. He was president of the Federation of Chemical Industries of Belgium from 1976 to 1979, president of the Federation of Belgian Companies from 1981 to 1984, president of the CEFIC (Conseil Européen de l'Industrie Chimique/European Chemical Industry Council) in 1991-1992 and a member of the management board of the European Round Table of Industrialists from 1991 to 2006.
- He was a member of the Board of Directors of Société Générale de Banque and then Fortis S.A./N.V. from 1977 to 2006. He was vice-president of the Board of Directors of UCB, a Belgian pharmaceutical company, where he worked from 1962 to 1984 and of which he was president of the Executive Board from 1975 to 1984 before joining Solvay. Daniel Janssen was president of the Executive Board of Solvay S.A. from June 2, 1986, to June 4, 1998, and then Chairman of the Board of Directors until May 9, 2006.
- He is a member of the management board of the Trilateral Commission. He is part of the Council of the Belgian American Educational Foundation and of INSEAD, and is also a member of the advisory board and is honorary president of the Solvay Business School.

Gilbert LENSSEN

- In the academic spectrum Professor Lenssen has formerly taught Business Environment at "The College of Europe" in Bruges and Warsaw, and is currently a Professor of Organisational Behaviour at Leiden University.
- As President of EABIS, Professor Lenssen directs the overall orientation and research content of the organization. His research and teaching areas include subjects in corporate social responsibility; the implications of globalisation for business, government and society; intercultural management, and organisational transformation.
- Professor Lenssen has worked as a business executive with British Petroleum (BP) across different disciplines in the United Kingdom, the United States, Germany, and Spain as well as other global roles.
- He graduated in political sciences and philosophy and holds an MBA from Case Western Reserve University Cleveland OH, and a PhD in social sciences from the Universities of Hamburg/Antwerp. He has written books and articles on management theory, management cultures, corporate responsibility and contemporary epistemology.
- On behalf of EABIS, Gilbert Lenssen is a member of the Editorial Board of the Corporate Governance Journal as well as a member of the European Foundation for Management Development (EFMD) Board. In addition to sitting on their Board, Professor Lenssen is also an EQUIS reviewer for EFMD. Moreover, he is engaged in several initiatives within Solvay and Leiden University.

Nicole NOTAT

- Founder and President of Vigeo, Nicole Notat was previously secretary general of the Confédération Française Démocratique du Travail (CFDT). She was president of the Unedic (unemployment insurance council) from 1992 to 1994 and from 1996 to 1998. A teacher by profession, Nicole Notat has played an active role in French and European trade unionism.

Martin ROMAN

- Martin Roman has been Chairman and CEO of ČEZ, a. s. since February 2004. Despite his young age (36), he has successfully held several management positions. He began his career in 1993 as the sales manager of Wolf Bergstrasse CR. There he was in charge of sales team development and logistics. Under his responsibility, the company rapidly became the leader in its market. He then joined Janka Radotin, where he became CEO in 1998, following the investment in the American company Lennox. In 2000, he became president of Skoda Holding, which he successfully restructured. He is repeating this performance at ČEZ, whose shares have gained 400% of their value since his arrival and which is today worth over $10 billion.

Arun SARIN

- Arun Sarin, age 52, has been Chief Executive Officer of Vodafone since July 2003, after joining the company in 1999. He also sits on the Nominations and Governance Committee.
- Arun Sarin joined Pacific Telesis Group in San Francisco in 1984 and has served in many executive positions in his 20 year career in telecommunications. He was a director of AirTouch from July 1995 and was President and Chief Operating Officer from February 1997 to June 1999. He was Chief Executive Officer for the Vodafone United States and Asia Pacific region until 15 April 2000, when he became a non-executive director.
- He has served as a director for The Gap, Inc, The Charles Schwab Corporation and Cisco Systems, Inc, and in June 2005 was appointed as a non-executive director to the Court of the Bank of England.

Ernest-Antoine SEILLIÈRE

- Graduate of the ENA and diplomat, Baron Ernest-Antoine Seillière was an advisor to the Cabinet of Jacques Chaban-Delmas in 1969, then in succession for Pierre Messmer, Maurice Schumann and Robert Galley. After a year at the Harvard Center for International Affairs, he joined the Wendel Group (CGIP) in 1976. He became CEO in 1987. WENDEL Investissement (ex-CGIP) was created in 2002 and he became president of the supervisory board in 2005. Since July 2005, he has been president of the Unice (Confederation of European Business). Previously, he presided over the MEDEF (Mouvement des Entreprises de France) from 1997 to 2005.
- Among his other mandates, he is president of the family board of Société Lorraine de Participations Sidérurgiques, president of the board of Oranje-Nassau Groep, and a member of the supervisory boards of Bureau Veritas, Editis Holding, Hermès International and Peugeot SA.

Pierre TAPIE

- Pierre Tapie holds an Engineer diploma from the Ecole Polytechnique of Paris (France), a Master of Science in Biochemistry and a Ph. D. in Biophysics from Paris XI Orsay University, and an MBA from INSEAD. He studied Theology at the Catholic Institute of Paris.
- He began his career at the French biotechnology group, Elf-Sanofi. Subsequently, for eleven years he was Dean of Purpan Graduate School of Engineering in Toulouse and CEO of Intellagri, the venture capital company. Committed to entrepreneurship, he coached the creation of 14 ventures. He has worked as a consultant in strategy for various companies. He has been teaching Business Ethics since 1990.
- Pierre Tapie became President of ESSEC Business School on September 1, 2001.
- Among his other current responsibilities, Pierre Tapie is Chairman of the French Federation of Private Business and Engineering Schools, Vice-Chairman of the National Conference of Engineering and Management Colleges, Member of the National Evaluation Commission of French Business Schools, and Member of the National Committee for Private higher education.
- Pierre Tapie is chevalier of the Legion of Honor, the highest French civil distinction. Married, he has four sons from 22 to 15.

Werner WENNING

- Werner Wenning has been Chairman of the Board of Management of Bayer AG since April 26, 2006.
- Born on October 21, 1946 in Leverkusen-Opladen, Wenning joined Bayer AG in Leverkusen as a commercial trainee on April 1, 1966. He then took a year's training in finance and accounting and worked for a further year in the Corporate Auditing Department. From 1970 to 1975 he established and managed the finance and accounting department of Bayer Industrial S.A., a company that had just been formed in Lima, Peru.
- On his return to Germany he worked for another three years in Corporate Auditing, returning to Lima in 1978 to become Managing Director and administrative head of the Peruvian company.
- In 1983, Wenning was appointed head of the staff department of what was then the Health Care Sector in Leverkusen. Three years

later he switched to the Plastics Business Group as head of marketing for thermoplastics, and in 1987 assumed responsibility for that business group's worldwide marketing operations.

- On April 1, 1991 he was seconded for a year to the Treuhandanstalt privatization agency in Berlin. In 1992 Wenning went abroad again, this time to Barcelona as Managing Director of Bayer Hispania Industrial S.A. and Senior Bayer Representative for Spain. In April 1996 he became head of Corporate Planning and Controlling in Leverkusen. He was appointed to the Board of Management of Bayer AG in February 1997.
- Wenning holds a number of offices outside Bayer. He is, for example: President of the German Chemical Industry Association (VCI), Frankfurt; Vice President of the Federation of German Industries (BDI), Berlin; a member of the supervisory board of Henkel KGaA.
- Werner Wenning is married with two grown-up daughters.

Yang Yuanqing

- Named CEO in 2001, Lenovo Chairman of the Board Yang Yuanqing played a key role in Lenovo's transformation into a truly global company, leading Lenovo to become the International Olympic Committee's worldwide partner in March 2004. Yang Yuanqing was also responsible for spearheading Lenovo's landmark acquisition of IBM's PC business in May 2005, fulfilling the company's internationalization strategy and making Lenovo the third-largest PC manufacturer worldwide.
- Born in 1964, Yang Yuanqing joined what was then called Legend Holdings in 1989, after he was awarded a master's degree from the Department of Computer Science at the University of Science and Technology of China. He was selected by the Chinese media as one of China's "Ten Star Entrepreneurs" and "Ten Most Valuable Managers" and was named by CCTV as a "Man of the Year" in 2004. Yang Yuanqing is a member of the National Youth Association Committee, director of China's Entrepreneurs' Association, a guest professor at the University of Science and Technology of China, and a member of the New York Stock Exchange International Advisory Committee.

Contents

Composé par MCP - N° 415908Z
Imprimé en France. - JOUVE, 11, bd de Sébastopol, 75001 PARIS